Treatise on purgatory
The dialogue

Treatise on Purgatory
The Dialogue

Saint Catherine of Genoa

Translated by Charlotte Balfour and Helen Irvine

Sheed and Ward
London

INTRODUCTION

Saint Catherine of Genoa was born in the Vicolo del Filo in that city, in 1447. She was of the great Guelph family of Fiesca, being the daughter of Giacomo Fiesca, at one time Viceroy of Naples, and granddaughter of Roberto Fiesca, whose brother was Pope Innocent IV. Another Fiesca was Pope Adrian V; for this family gave several princes to the Church and many bold and skilful warriors and statesmen to the state. The saint's mother, Francesca de Negro, was likewise of aristocratic birth.

Catherine, who was one of five children, was brought up piously. Her earliest biography, written by the priest Cattaneo Marabotto, who was her confessor in her latter years, and by her friend Ettore Vernazza, relates that her penances were remarkable from the time she was eight, and that she received the gift of prayer in her thirteenth year. When she was thirteen she declared to her confessor her wish to enter the convent of Santa Maria delle Grazie, in Genoa, a house of Augustinian Canonesses of the Lateran in which her elder sister Limbania had already taken the veil. He pointed out to her that she was still very young and that the life of a religious was hard, but she met his objections with a "prudence and zeal" which seemed to him "not human but supernatural and divine". So he visited the convent of her predilection, to which he was confessor, and urged the mothers to accept her as a novice. But they were obdurate against transgressing their custom by receiving so young a girl. Catherine's disappointment gave her "great pain, but she hoped the Lord Almighty would not forsake her".

She grew up to be very lovely: "taller than most women, her head well proportioned, her face rather long but singularly beautiful and well shaped, her complexion fair and in the flower of her youth rubicund, her nose long rather than short, her eyes dark and her forehead high and broad; every part of her body was well formed." About the time she failed to enter the convent, or a little later, her father died, and his power and possessions passed to her eldest brother Giacomo. Wishing to compose the differences between the factions into which the principal families of Genoa were divided— differences which had long entailed cruel, distracting and wearing strife—Giacomo Fiesca formed the project of marrying his young sister to Giuliano Adorni, son of the head of a powerful Ghibelline family. He obtained his mother's support for his plan, and found Giuliano willing to accept the beautiful, noble and rich bride proposed to him; as for Catherine herself, she would not refuse this cross laid on her at the command of her mother and eldest brother. On the 13th of January, 1463, at the age of sixteen, she was married to Giuliano Adorni.

He is described as a man of "strange and recalcitrant nature" who wasted his substance on disorderly living. Catherine, living with him in his fine house in the Piazza Sant' Agnete, at first entirely refused to adopt his worldly ways, and lived "like a hermit", never going out except to hear Mass. But when she had thus spent five years, she yielded to the remonstrances of her family, and for the next five years practised a certain commerce with the world, partaking of the pleasures customary among the women of her class but never falling into sin. Increasingly she was irked and wearied by her husband's lack of spiritual sympathy with her, and by the distractions which kept her from God.

Her conversion is dated from the eve of St. Bernard, 1474, when she visited the church of St. Bernard, in Genoa, and prayed, so intolerable had life in the world become to her, that she might have an illness which would keep her three months in bed. Her prayer was not granted but her longing to leave the world persisted. Two days later she visited her sister Limbania in the convent of Santa Maria delle Grazie, and at Limbania's instance returned there on the morrow to make her confession to the nuns' confessor. Suddenly, as she was kneeling down at the confessional, "her heart was wounded by a dart of God's immense love, and she had a clear vision of her own wretchedness and faults and the most high goodness of God. She fell to the ground, all but swooning", and from her heart rose the unuttered cry, "No more of the world for me! No more sin!" The confessor was at this moment called away, and when he came back she could speak again, and asked and obtained his leave to postpone her confession.

Then she hurried home, to shut herself up in the most secluded room in the house, and for several days she stayed there absorbed by consciousness of her own wretchedness and of God's mercy in warning her. She had a vision of Our Lord, weighed down by His Cross and covered with blood, and she cried aloud, "O Lord, I will never sin again; if need be, I will make public confession of my sins." After a time, she was inspired with a desire for Holy Communion which she fulfilled on the feast of the Annunciation.

She now entered on a life of prayer and penance. She obtained from her husband a promise, which he kept, to live with her as a brother. She made strict rules for herself—to avert her eyes from sights of the world, to speak no useless words, to eat only what was necessary for life, to sleep as little as possible and on a bed in which she put briars and thistles, to wear a rough hair shirt. Every day she spent six hours in prayer. She rigorously mortified her affections and will.

Soon, guided by the Ladies of Mercy, she was devoting herself to the care of the sick poor. In her plain dress she would go through the streets and byways of Genoa, looking for poor people who were ill, and when she found them she tended them and washed and mended their filthy rags. Often she visited the hospital of St. Lazarus, which harboured incurables so diseased as to be horrible to the sight and smell, many of them embittered. In Catherine they aroused not disgust but charity; she met their insults with unfailing gentleness.

Her earliest biography gives details of her religious practices. From the time of her conversion she hungered insatiably for the Holy Eucharist, and the priests admitted her to the privilege, very rare in that period, of daily communion. For twenty-three years, beginning in the third year after her conversion, she fasted completely throughout Lent and Advent, except that at long intervals she drank a glass of water mixed with salt and vinegar to remind herself of the drink offered to Our Lord on the cross, and during these fasts she enjoyed exceptional health and vigour. For twenty-five years after her conversion she had no spiritual director except Our Lord Himself. Then, when she had fallen into the illness which afflicted the last ten years of her life, she felt the need for human help, and a priest named Cattaneo Marabotto, who had a position of authority in the hospital in which she was then working, became her confessor.

Some years after her conversion her husband was received into the third order of St. Francis, and afterwards he helped her in her works of mercy.

The time came when the directors of the great hospital in Genoa asked Catherine to superintend the care of the sick in this institution. She accepted, and hired near the hospital a poor house in which she and her husband lived out the rest of their days. Her prayers were still long and regular and her raptures frequent, but she so arranged that neither her devotions nor her ecstasies interfered with her care of the sick. Although she was humbly submissive even to the hospital servants, the directors saw the value of her work and appointed her rector of the hospital with unlimited powers.

In 1497 she nursed her husband through his last illness. In his will he extolled her virtues and left her all his possessions.

Mrs. Charlotte Balfour underlined in her copy of the saint's works an indicative extract from her teaching. "We should not wish for anything but what comes to us from moment to moment," Saint Catherine told her spiritual children, "exercising ourselves none the less for good. For he who would not thus exercise himself, and await what God sends, would tempt God. When we have done what good we can, let us accept all that happens to us by Our Lord's ordinance, and let us unite ourselves to it by our will. Who tastes what it is to rest in union with God will seem to himself to have won to Paradise even in this life."

She was still only fifty-three years old when she fell ill, worn out by her life of ecstasies, her burning love for God, labour for her fellow creatures and her privations; during her last ten years on earth she suffered much. She died on the 15th of September, 1510, at the age of sixty-three. The public cult rendered to her was declared legitimate on the 6th of April, 1675. The process for her canonization was instituted by the directors of the hospital in Genoa where she had worked. Her heroic virtue and the authenticity of many miracles attributed to her having been proved, the bull for her canonization was issued by Clement XII on the 30th of April, 1737.

Saint Catherine's authorship of the *Treatise on Purgatory* has never been disputed. But Baron von Hügel in his monumental work the *Mystical Element in Religion as Studied in Saint Catherine of Genoa and her Friends* concludes convincingly, after a meticulous examination of the *Dialogue of the Blessed and Seraphic Saint Catherine of Genoa*, that its author was Battista Vernazza: "The entire *Dialogue* then is the work of Battista Vernazza." Thus this work is not, as has been thought, the saint's spiritual autobiography, nor indeed does it ever claim to be other

than what it is, her spiritual biography. It is the life
of her soul, dramatised by a younger woman who had
known her and her intimates, who had a singular devotion to her, and who was peculiarly qualified to understand her experience.

Baron von Hügel believed that Saint Catherine first
became acquainted with the Genoese notary Ettore
Vernazza during the epidemic in Genoa in 1493, that
is nineteen years after her conversion, when she was
forty-six years old and he in his early twenties. She wrote
of "a great compassion he had conceived when still very
young, at the time the pestilence raged in Genoa, when
he used to go about to help the poor". Von Hügel
describes him, after profound study of his life and works,
as "a man of fine and keen, deep and world-embracing
mind and heart, of an overflowing, ceaseless activity,
and of a will of steel". He was "the most intimate,
certainly the most perceptive of Catherine's disciples"
and with Cattaneo Marabotto wrote the earliest life
of her. In 1496 he married Bartolomea Ricci, and
they had three daughters of whom the eldest, Tommasa,
had Saint Catherine for godmother.

Little Tommasa was a sensitive, loving, bright child
with a turn for writing, as she shewed in a few simple
lines of verse which she wrote to her "most holy pro-
tectress" and "adored mother" when she was only ten.
Was she addressing her godmother, or her mother in the
flesh who died not long afterwards? Her father, after
his wife's death, sent her and her little sister Catetta to
board in that convent of Augustinian canonesses in
which Saint Catherine had not been allowed to take the
veil. Perhaps the nuns had been taught by the saint
that very young girls may have a true vocation to
religion, for Tommasa was only thirteen when, on the
24th of June, 1510, she received in their house the
habit of an Augustinian Canoness of the Lateran and
changed her name to Battista. She spent all the rest
of her ninety years on earth in that convent in Genoa.

Twelve weeks after her reception Saint Catherine died, and Baron von Hügel tentatively identifies Battista with an unnamed nun to whom, and to six other friends and disciples of the saint, Battista's father among them, "intimations and communications of her passage and instant complete union with God" were vouchsafed at the moment of her death.

Battista's literary remains include many letters, poetry —both spiritual canticles and sonnets, and several volumes of spiritual dissertations in which are "all but endless parallels and illustrations" to the teachings of Saint Catherine. She wrote also three sets of *Colloquies*, and in one of them relates certain of her own spiritual experiences. In all her writings, but especially in these narrations, Baron von Hügel notes the influence of Catherine's doctrine and spiritual practices.

The *Dialogue* reproduces the incidents of the saint's spiritual life as these are recorded in her earliest biography, and its doctrine is that embodied in the *Treatise on Purgatory* and in her recorded sayings, from which even its language is in large part derived. That its matter has passed through another mind, Battista's, gives it an added interest: there is the curious, vivid dramatization; there is, in some passages, a poignant and individual quality; and there is an insight which proves that Battista herself was also a mystic, one who had spent all her days in the spiritual companionship of Saint Catherine. We are shewn not only the saint but also her reflection in the mirror which was Battista's mind. "A person", says Von Hügel, speaking of Battista at the time when she wrote the *Dialogue*, "living now thirty-eight years after Catherine's death, in an environment of a kind to preserve her memory green. . . . Battista, the god-daughter of the heroine of the work, and the eldest, devoted daughter of the chief contributor to the already extant biography; a contemplative with a deep interest in, and much practical experience of, the kind of spirituality to be portrayed and the sort of literature required;

a nun during thirty-eight years in the very convent where Catherine's sister, one of its foundresses, had lived and died, and where Catherine herself had desired to live and where her conversion had taken place."

The *Dialogue*, long generally accepted as Catherine's own account of her spiritual life, has been allowed by the highest authorities to embody, with her *Treatise on Purgatory*, the saint's doctrine. These two treatises and the earliest biography, translated into several languages, spread that doctrine and devotion to her throughout the Catholic world in the centuries between her death and her canonization. The bull which canonized her alludes to the *Dialogue* as an exposition of her doctrine: "In her admirable *Dialogue* she depicts the dangers to which a soul bound by the flesh is exposed."

The Vicomte Théodore Marie de Bussierne includes the *Dialogue* with the *Treatise on Purgatory* in his translation into French of the saint's works, published in 1860. It was from this translation that Mrs. Charlotte Balfour translated the first half of the *Dialogue* into English. She meant to make an English version of all the saint's works but had worked only on the *Dialogue* at the time of her death. Her work has been carefully collated with the Italian original and revised where necessary, the edition used being that included in the beautiful *Life and Works* of Saint Catherine which was printed in Rome in 1737, the year of her canonization, by Giovanni Battista de Caporali, and dedicated to Princess Vittoria Altoviti de' Corsini, the Pope's niece. As here printed, the whole *Dialogue* may be regarded as translated from Battista Venazza's original work. Mrs. Balfour would certainly have wished to acknowledge her debt to Monsieur de Bussierne's French version. The latter part of the *Dialogue* and the whole *Treatise on Purgatory* have been directly translated from the 1737 Italian edition of the saint's works.

Saint Catherine's earliest biography concludes with the following words:

"It remains for us to pray the Lord, of His great goodness and by the intercession of this glorious Seraphin, to give us His love abundantly, that we may not cease to grow in virtue, and may at last win to eternal beatitude with God who lives and reigns for ever and ever."

H.D.I.

CONTENTS

TREATISE ON PURGATORY

How by Comparing it to the Divine Fire which she Felt in Herself, this Soul Understood what Purgatory was like and how the Souls there were Tormented.[1]

CHAPTER I

The state of the souls who are in Purgatory, how they are exempt from all self-love.

This holy Soul[2] found herself, while still in the flesh, placed by the fiery love of God in Purgatory, which burnt her, cleansing whatever in her needed cleansing, to the end that when she passed from this life she might be presented to the sight of God, her dear Love. By means of this loving fire, she understood in her soul the state of the souls of the faithful who are placed in Purgatory to purge them of all the rust and stains of sin of which they have not rid themselves in this life. And since this Soul, placed by the divine fire in this loving Purgatory, was united to that divine love and content with all that was wrought in her, she understood the state of the souls who are in Purgatory. And she said:

The souls who are in Purgatory cannot, as I understand, choose but be there, and this is by God's ordinance who therein has done justly. They cannot turn their thoughts back to themselves, nor can they say, "Such sins I have committed for which I deserve to be here", nor, "I would that I had not committed them for then I would go now to Paradise", nor, "That one will leave sooner

---

[1] The chapter headings are unlikely to have been written by Saint Catherine, who would hardly refer to herself as a saint as do the headings to Chapter IV and IX.

[2] At least the word "holy" and perhaps all this introductory paragraph were probably added by whoever wrote the chapter headings.

than I", nor, "I will leave sooner than he". They can have neither of themselves nor of others any memory, whether of good or evil, whence they would have greater pain than they suffer ordinarily. So happy are they to be within God's ordinance, and that He should do all which pleases Him, as it pleases Him that in their greatest pain they cannot think of themselves. They see only the working of the divine goodness, which leads man to itself mercifully, so that he no longer sees aught of the pain or good which may befall him. Nor would these souls be in pure charity if they could see that pain or good. They cannot see that they are in pain because of their sins; that sight they cannot hold in their minds because in it there would be an active imperfection, which cannot be where no actual sin can be.

Only once, as they pass from this life, do they see the cause of the Purgatory they endure; never again do they see it for in another sight of it there would be self. Being then in charity from which they cannot now depart by any actual fault, they can no longer will nor desire save with the pure will of pure charity. Being in that fire of Purgatory, they are within the divine ordinance, which is pure charity, and in nothing can they depart thence for they are deprived of the power to sin as of the power to merit.

CHAPTER II

What is the joy of the souls in Purgatory. A comparison to shew how they see God ever more and more. The difficulty of speaking of this state.

I believe no happiness can be found worthy to be compared with that of a soul in Purgatory except that of the saints in Paradise; and day by day this happiness grows as God flows into these souls, more and more as the hindrance to His entrance is consumed. Sin's rust is the hindrance, and the fire burns the rust away so that more and more the soul opens itself up to the divine inflowing. A thing which is covered cannot respond to the sun's rays, not because of any defect in the sun, which is shining all the time, but because the cover is an obstacle; if the cover be burnt away, this thing is open to the sun; more and more as the cover is consumed does it respond to the rays of the sun.

It is in this way that rust, which is sin, covers souls, and in Purgatory is burnt away by fire; the more it is consumed, the more do the souls respond to God, the true sun. As the rust lessens and the soul is opened up to the divine ray, happiness grows; until the time be accomplished the one wanes and the other waxes. Pain however does not lessen but only the time for which pain is endured. As for will: never can the souls say these pains are pains, so contented are they with God's ordaining with which, in pure charity, their will is united.

But, on the other hand, they endure a pain so extreme that no tongue can be found to tell it, nor could the mind understand its least pang if God by special grace did not shew so much. Which least pang God of His grace shewed to this Soul, but with her tongue she cannot say what it is. This sight which the Lord revealed to me has never since left my mind and I will tell what I can of it. They will understand whose mind God deigns to open.

CHAPTER III

Separation from God is the chief punishment of Purgatory. Wherein Purgatory differs from Hell.

All the pains of Purgatory arise from original or actual sin. God created the soul pure, simple and clean of all stain of sin, with a certain beatific instinct towards

Himself whence original sin, which the soul finds in itself, draws it away, and when actual is added to original sin the soul is drawn yet further away. The further it departs from its beatific instinct, the more malignant it becomes because it corresponds less to God.

There can be no good save by participation in God, who meets the needs of irrational creatures as He wills and has ordained, never failing them, and answers to a rational soul in the measure in which He finds it cleansed of sin's hindrance. When therefore a soul has come near to the pure and clear state in which it was created, its beatific instinct discovers itself and grows unceasingly, so impetuously and with such fierce charity (drawing it to its last end) that any hindrance seems to this soul a thing past bearing. The more it sees, the more extreme is its pain.

Because the souls in Purgatory are without the guilt of sin, there is no hindrance between them and God except their pain, which holds them back so that they cannot reach perfection. Clearly they see the grievousness of every least hindrance in their way, and see too that their instinct is hindered by a necessity of justice: thence is born a raging fire, like that of Hell save that guilt is lacking to it. Guilt it is which makes the will of the damned in Hell malignant, on whom God does not bestow His goodness and who remain therefore in desperate ill will, opposed to the will of God.

CHAPTER IV

Of the state of the souls in Hell and of the difference between them and those in Purgatory. Reflections of this saint on those who are careless of their salvation.

Hence it is manifest that there is perversity of will, contrary to the will of God, where the guilt is known and ill will persists, and that the guilt of those who have passed with ill will from this life to Hell is not remitted, nor can be since they may no longer change the will with which they have passed out of this life, in which passage the soul is made stable in good or evil in accordance with its deliberate will. As it is written, *Ubi te invenero*, that is in the hour of death, with the will to sin or dissatisfaction with sin or repentance for sin, *Ibi te judicabo*. Of which judgment there is afterwards no remission, as I will shew:

After death free will can never return, for the will is fixed as it was at the moment of death. Because the souls in Hell were found at the moment of death to have in them the will to sin, they bear the guilt throughout eternity, suffering not indeed the pains they merit but such pains as they endure, and these without end. But the souls in Purgatory bear only pain, for their guilt was wiped away at the moment of their death when they were found to be ill content with their sins and repentant for their offences against divine goodness. Therefore their pain is finite and its time ever lessening, as has been said.

O misery beyond all other misery, the greater that human blindness takes it not into account!

The pain of the damned is not infinite in quantity because the dear goodness of God sheds the ray of His mercy even in Hell. For man dead in sin merits infinite pain for an infinite time, but God's mercy has allotted infinity to him only in time and has determined the quantity of his pain; in justice God could have given him more pain.

O how dangerous is sin committed in malice! Hardly does a man repent him thereof, and without repentance he will bear its guilt for as long as he perseveres, that is for as long as he wills a sin committed or wills to sin again.

CHAPTER V

Of the peace and the joy there are in Purgatory.

The souls in Purgatory have wills accordant in all things with the will of God, who therefore sheds on them His goodness, and they, as far as their will goes, are happy and cleansed of all their sin. As for guilt, these cleansed souls are as they were when God created them, for God forgives their guilt immediately who have passed from this life ill content with their sins, having confessed all they have committed and having the will to commit no more. Only the rust of sin is left them and from this they cleanse themselves by pain in the fire. Thus cleansed of all guilt and united in will to God, they see Him clearly in the degree in which He makes Himself known to them, and see too how much it imports to enjoy Him and that souls have been created for this end. Moreover, they are brought to so uniting a conformity with God, and are drawn to Him in such wise, His natural instinct towards souls working in them, that neither arguments nor figures nor examples can make the thing clear as the mind knows it to be in effect and as by inner feeling it is understood to be. I will, however, make one comparison which comes to my mind.

CHAPTER VI

A comparison to shew with what violence and what love the souls in Purgatory desire to enjoy God.

If in all the world there were but one loaf of bread to feed the hunger of all creatures, and if they were satisfied by the sight of it alone, then since man, if he be healthy, has an instinct to eat, his hunger, if he neither ate nor sickened nor died, would grow unceasingly for his instinct to eat would not lessen. Knowing that there was only that loaf to satisfy him and that without it he must still be hungry, he would be in unbearable pain. All the more if he went near that loaf and could not see it, would his natural craving for it be strengthened; his instinct would fix his desire wholly on that loaf which held all that could content him; at this point, if he were sure he would never see the loaf again, he would be in Hell. Thus are the souls of the damned from whom any hope of ever seeing their bread, which is God, the true Saviour, has been taken away. But the souls in Purgatory have the hope of seeing their bread and wholly satisfying themselves therewith. Therefore they suffer hunger and endure pain in that measure in which they will be able to satisfy themselves with the bread which is Jesus Christ, true God and Saviour and our Love.

CHAPTER VII

Of God's admirable wisdom in making Purgatory and Hell.

As the clean and purified spirit can find rest only in God, having been created for this end, so there is no place save Hell for the soul in sin, for whose end Hell was ordained by God. When the soul as it leaves the body is in mortal sin, then, in the instant in which spirit and body are separated, the soul goes to the place ordained for it, unguided save by the nature of its sin. And if at that moment the soul were bound by no ordinance proceeding from God's justice, it would go to a yet greater hell than that in which it abides, for it would be outside His ordinance, in which divine mercy has part so that God gives the soul less pain than it deserves. The soul, finding no other place to hand nor any holding less evil for it, casts itself by God's ordinance into Hell as into its proper place.

To return to our matter which is the Purgatory of the soul separated from the body when it is no longer clean as it was created. Seeing in itself the impediment which can be taken away only by means of Purgatory, it casts itself therein swiftly and willingly. Were there not the ordinance it thus obeys, one fit to rid it of its encumbrance, it would in that instant beget within itself a hell worse than Purgatory, for it would see that because of that impediment it could not draw near to God, its end. So much does God import that Purgatory in comparison counts not at all, for all that it is, as has been said, like Hell. But compared to God, it appears almost nothing.

CHAPTER VIII

Of the necessity of Purgatory. How terrible it is.

When I look at God, I see no gate to Paradise, and yet because God is all mercy he who wills enters there. God stands before us with open arms to receive us into His glory. But well I see the divine essence to be of such purity, greater far than can be imagined, that the soul in which there is even the least note of imperfection would rather cast itself into a thousand Hells than find itself thus stained in the presence of the Divine Majesty. Therefore the soul, understanding that Purgatory has been ordained to take away those stains, casts itself therein, and seems to itself to have found great mercy in that it can rid itself there of the impediment which is the stain of sin.

No tongue can tell nor explain, no mind understand, the grievousness of Purgatory. But I, though I see that there is in Purgatory as much pain as in Hell, yet see the soul which has the least stain of imperfection accepting Purgatory, as I have said, as though it were a mercy, and holding its pains of no account as compared with the least stain which hinders a soul in its love. I seem to see that the pain which souls in Purgatory endure because of whatever in them displeases God, that is what they have wilfully done against His so great goodness, is greater than any other pain they feel in Purgatory. And this is because, being in grace, they see the truth and the grievousness of the hindrance which stays them from drawing near to God.

CHAPTER IX

How God and the souls in Purgatory look at each other. The saint acknowledges that in speaking of these matters she cannot express herself.

All these things which I have surely in mind, in so much as in this life I have been able to understand them, are, as compared with what I have said, extreme in their greatness. Beside them, all the sights and sounds and justice and truths of this world seem to me lies and nothingness. I am left confused because I cannot find words extreme enough for these things.

I perceive there to be so much conformity between God and the soul that when He sees it in the purity in which His Divine Majesty created it He gives it a burning love, which draws it to Himself, which is strong enough to destroy it, immortal though it be, and which causes it to be so transformed in God that it sees itself as though it were none other than God. Unceasingly He draws it to Himself and breathes fire into it, never letting it go until He has led it to the state whence it came forth, that is to the pure cleanliness in which it was created.

When with its inner sight the soul sees itself drawn by God with such loving fire, then it is melted by the heat of the glowing love for God, its most dear Lord, which it feels overflowing it. And it sees by the divine light that God does not cease from drawing it, nor from leading it, lovingly and with much care and unfailing foresight, to its full perfection, doing this of His pure love. But the soul, being hindered by sin, cannot go whither God draws it; it cannot follow the uniting look with which He would draw it to Himself. Again the soul perceives the grievousness of being held back from seeing the divine light; the soul's instinct too, being drawn by that uniting look, craves to be unhindered. I say that it is the sight of these things which begets in the souls the pain they feel in Purgatory. Not that they make account of their pain; most great though it be, they deem it a far less evil than to find themselves going against the will of God, whom they clearly see to be on fire with extreme and pure love for them.

Strongly and unceasingly this love draws the soul with that uniting look, as though it had nought else than this to do. Could the soul who understood find a worse Purgatory in which to rid itself sooner of all the hindrance in its way, it would swiftly fling itself therein, driven by the conforming love between itself and God.

CHAPTER X

How God uses Purgatory to make the soul wholly pure. The soul acquires in Purgatory a purity so great that were it well for it still to stay there after it had been purged of sin, it would no longer suffer.

I see, too, certain rays and shafts of light which go out from that divine love towards the soul and are penetrating and strong enough to seem as though they must destroy not only the body but the soul too, were that possible. Two works are wrought by these rays, the first purification and the second destruction.

Look at gold: the more you melt it, the better it becomes; you could melt it until you had destroyed in it every imperfection. Thus does fire work on material things. The soul cannot be destroyed in so far as it is in God, but in so far as it is in itself it can be destroyed; the more it is purified, the more is self destroyed within it, until at last it is pure in God.

When gold has been purified up to twenty-four carats, it can no longer be consumed by any fire; not gold itself but only dross can be burnt away. Thus the divine fire works in the soul: God holds the soul in the fire until its every imperfection is burnt away and it is brought to perfection, as it were to the purity of twenty-four carats, each soul however according to its own degree. When the soul has been purified it stays wholly in God, having nothing of self in it; its being is in God who has led this cleansed soul to Himself; it can suffer no more for nothing is left in it to be burnt away; were it held in the fire when it has thus been cleansed, it would feel no pain. Rather the fire of divine love would be to it like eternal life and in no way contrary to it.

CHAPTER XI

Of the desire of souls in Purgatory to be wholly cleansed of the stains of their sins. The wisdom of God who suddenly hides their faults from these souls.

The soul was created as well conditioned as it is capable of being for reaching perfection if it live as God has ordained and do not foul itself with any stain of sin. But having fouled itself by original sin, it loses its gifts and graces and lies dead, nor can it rise again save by

God's means. And when God, by baptism, has raised it from the dead, it is still prone to evil, inclining and being led to actual sin unless it resist. And thus it dies again.

Then God by another special grace raises it again, yet it stays so sullied and so turned to self that all the divine workings of which we have spoken are needed to recall it to its first state in which God created it; without them it could never get back thither. And when the soul finds itself on the road back to its first state, its need to be transformed in God kindles in it a fire so great that this is its Purgatory. Not that it can look upon this as Purgatory, but its instinct to God, aflame and thwarted, makes Purgatory.

A last act of love is done by God without help from man. So many hidden imperfections are in the soul that, did it see them, it would live in despair. But in the state of which we have spoken they are all burnt away, and only when they have gone does God shew them to the soul, so that it may see that divine working which kindles the fire of love in which its imperfections have been burnt away.

CHAPTER XII

How suffering in Purgatory is coupled with joy.

Know that what man deems perfection in himself is in God's sight faulty, for all the things a man does which he sees or feels or means or wills or remembers to have a perfect seeming are wholly fouled and sullied unless he acknowledge them to be from God. If a work is to be perfect it must be wrought in us but not chiefly by us, for God's works must be done in Him and not wrought chiefly by man.

Such works are those last wrought in us by God of His

pure and clean love, by Him alone without merit of ours, and so penetrating are they and such fire do they kindle in the soul, that the body which wraps it seems to be consumed as in a furnace never to be quenched until death. It is true that love for God which fills the soul to overflowing, gives it, so I see it, a happiness beyond what can be told, but this happiness takes not one pang from the pain of the souls in Purgatory. Rather the love of these souls, finding itself hindered, causes their pain; and the more perfect is the love of which God has made them capable, the greater is their pain.

So that the souls in Purgatory enjoy the greatest happiness and endure the greatest pain; the one does not hinder the other.

CHAPTER XIII

The souls in Purgatory are no longer in a state to acquire merit. How these souls look on the charity exercised for them in the world.

If the souls in Purgatory could purge themselves by contrition, they would pay all their debt in one instant, such blazing vehemence would their contrition have in the clear light shed for them on the grievousness of being hindered from reaching their end and the love of God.

Know surely that not the least farthing of payment is remitted to those souls, for thus has it been determined by God's justice. So much for what God does; as for what the souls do, they can no longer choose for themselves, nor can they see or will, save as God wills, for thus has it been determined for them.

And if any alms be done them by those who are in the world to lessen the time of their pain, they cannot turn with affection to contemplate the deed, saving as it is weighed in the most just scales of the divine will. They leave all in God's hands who pays Himself as His infinite goodness pleases. If they could turn to contemplate the alms except as it is within the divine will, there would be self in what they did and they would lose sight of God's will, which would make a Hell for them. Therefore they await immovably all that God gives them, whether pleasure and happiness or pain, and never more can they turn their eyes back to themselves.

CHAPTER XIV

Of the submission of the souls in Purgatory to God's will.

So intimate with God are the souls in Purgatory and so changed to His will, that in all things they are content with His most holy ordinance. And if a soul were brought to see God when it had still a trifle of which to purge itself, a great injury would be done it. For since pure love and supreme justice could not brook that stained soul, and to bear with its presence would not befit God, it would suffer a torment worse than ten purgatories. To see God when full satisfaction had not yet been made Him, even if the time of purgation lacked but the twinkling of an eye, would be unbearable to that soul. It would sooner go to a thousand hells, to rid itself of the little rust still clinging to it, than stand in the divine presence when it was not yet wholly cleansed.

CHAPTER XV

Reproaches which the souls in Purgatory make to people in the world.

And so that blessed[1] soul, seeing the aforesaid things by the divine light, said: "I would fain send up a cry so loud that it would put fear in all men on the earth. I would say to them: 'Wretches, why do you let yourselves be thus blinded by the world, you whose need is so great and grievous, as you will know at the moment of death, and who make no provision for it whatsoever?'

"You have all taken shelter beneath hope in God's mercy, which is, you say, very great, but you see not that this great goodness of God will judge you for having gone against the will of so good a Lord. His goodness should constrain you to do all His will, not give you hope in ill-doing, for His justice cannot fail but in one way or another must needs be fully satisfied.

"Cease to hug yourselves, saying: 'I will confess my sins and then receive plenary indulgence, and at that moment I shall be purged of all my sins and thus shall be saved.' Think of the confession and the contrition needed for that plenary indulgence, so hardly come by that, if you knew, you would tremble in great fear, more sure you would never win it than that you ever could."

CHAPTER XVI

This Soul shews again how the sufferings of the souls in Purgatory are no hindrance at all to their peace and their joy.

I see the souls suffer the pains of Purgatory having before their eyes two works of God.

[1] This epithet, and perhaps all this sentence down to "said", have probably been added by an editor.

First, they see themselves suffering pain willingly, and as they consider their own deserts and acknowledge how they have grieved God, it seems to them that He has shewn them great mercy, for if His goodness had not tempered justice with mercy, making satisfaction with the precious blood of Jesus Christ, one sin would deserve a thousand perpetual hells. And therefore the souls suffer pain willingly, and would not lighten it by one pang, knowing that they most fully deserve it and that it has been well ordained, and they no more complain of God, as far as their will goes, than if they were in eternal life.

The second work they see is the happiness they feel as they contemplate God's ordinance and the love and mercy with which He works on the soul.

In one instant God imprints these two sights on their minds, and because they are in grace they are aware of these sights and understand them as they are, in the measure of their capacity. Thus a great happiness is granted them which never fails; rather it grows as they draw nearer God. These souls see these sights neither in nor of themselves but in God, on whom they are far more intent than on the pains they suffer, and of whom they make far greater account, beyond all comparison, than of their pains. For every glimpse which can be had of God exceeds any pain or joy a man can feel. Albeit, however, it exceeds the pain and joy of these souls, it lessens them by not a tittle.

CHAPTER XVII

She concludes by applying all she has said of the souls in Purgatory to what she feels and has proved in her own soul.

This form of purgation, which I see in the souls in Purgatory, I feel in my own mind. In the last two years I have felt it most; every day I feel and see it more clearly. I see my soul within this body as in a purgatory, formed as is the true Purgatory and like it, but so measured that the body can bear with it and not die; yet little by little it grows until the body die.

I see my spirit estranged from all things, even things spiritual, which can feed it, such as gaiety, delight and consolation, and without the power so to enjoy anything, spiritual or temporal, by will or mind or memory, as to let me say one thing contents me more than another.

Inwardly I find myself as it were besieged. All things by which spiritual or bodily life is refreshed have, little by little, been taken from my inner self, which knows, now they are gone, that they fed and comforted. But so hateful and abhorrent are these things, as they are known to the spirit, that they all go never to return. This is because of the spirit's instinct to rid itself of whatever hinders its perfection; so ruthless is it that to fulfil its purpose it would all but cast itself into Hell. Therefore it ever deprives the inner man of all on which it can feed, besieging it so cunningly that it lets not the least atom of imperfection pass unseen and unabhorred.

As for my outer man, it too, since the spirit does not respond to it, is so besieged that it finds nothing to refresh it on the earth if it follow its human instinct. No comfort is left it save God, who works all this by love and very mercifully in satisfaction of His justice. To perceive this gives my outer man great peace and happiness, but happiness which neither lessens my pain nor weakens the siege. Yet no pain could ever be inflicted on me so great that I would wish to depart from the divine ordinance. I neither leave my prison nor seek to go forth from it: let God do what is needed! My happiness is that God be satisfied, nor could I suffer a worse pain than that of going outside God's ordinance, so just I see Him to be and so very merciful.

All these things of which I have spoken are what I see and, as it were, touch, but I cannot find fit words

to say as much as I would of them. Nor can I say rightly
what I have told of the work done in me, which I have
felt spiritually. I have told it however.

The prison in which I seem to myself to be is the world,
my chains the body, and it is my soul enlightened by
grace which knows the grievousness of being held down
or kept back and thus hindered from pursuing its end.
This gives my soul great pain for it is very tender. By
God's grace it receives a certain dignity which makes
it like unto God; nay, rather He lets it share His
goodness so that it becomes one with Him. And since
it is impossible that God suffer pain, this immunity
too befalls the souls who draw near Him; the nearer
they come to Him, the more they partake of what is
His.

Therefore to be hindered on its way, as it is, causes
the soul unbearable pain. The pain and the hindrance
wrest it from its first natural state, which by grace is
revealed to it, and finding itself deprived of what it is
able to receive, it suffers a pain more or less great
according to the measure of its esteem for God. The
more the soul knows God, the more it esteems Him and
the more sinless it becomes, so that the hindrance in
its way grows yet more terrible to it, above all because
the soul which is unhindered and wholly recollected
in God knows Him as He truly is.

As the man who would let himself be killed rather
than offend God feels death and its pain, but is given
by the light of God a zeal which causes him to rate
divine honour above bodily death, so the soul who knows
God's ordinance rates it above all possible inner and
outer torments, terrible though they may be, for this
is a work of God who surpasses all that can be felt or
imagined. Moreover God when He occupies a soul,
in however small a degree, keeps it wholly busied over
His Majesty so that nothing else counts for it. Thus it
loses all which is its own, and can of itself neither see
nor speak nor know loss or pain. But, as I have already

said clearly, it knows all in one instant when it leaves this life.

Finally and in conclusion, let us understand that God who is best and greatest causes all that is of man to be lost, and that Purgatory cleanses it away.

END OF THE TREATISE ON PURGATORY

DIALOGUE
OF
SAINT CATHERINE FIESCHI ADORNA

*Spoken by the Soul, the Body, Self-Love, the Spirit, Natural
Man and the Lord God*

NOTE ON THE *NOMENCLATURE OF THE CHARACTERS* IN THE DIALOGUE

The author, Battista Vernazza varies the characters
in the *Dialogue*, sometimes changes their names, and
sometimes applies the same name first to one and
then to a slightly different character: this may be
confusing.

The first nine chapters of Part I contain colloquies
between the Soul, the Body and Self-Love, and the
ensuing chapters others between the Soul and Natural
Man (*Umanità*) which in truth introduce no new character
for in them Natural Man is identical with the Body.
"I will be in the grave," he says in Chapter XIV,
alluding to the time after death, and in Chapter XVI
he says, "I am an animal body." Yet sometimes, as in
Chapter XVIII, Battista is mindful that natural man
has a soul as well as a body and makes her Natural Man
personify the complete human being whom she much
oftener calls the creature. In Chapter XIV a new
character appears, the Spirit, who is not to be confused
with the Holy Ghost or the Spirit of God, but is for
Battista a part of man, usually a part purer and less
complex than the Soul because neither tempted nor prone
to sin but singly intent on God. The distinction is perhaps
that between the soul in a state of supernatural grace,
whom she called the Spirit, and the soul still in its merely
natural disposition, whom she called the Soul. Yet

sometimes, as in Chapter XVI, the Spirit is completely identified with the soul in its natural state.

In the first two chapters of Part II, Body and Natural Man are the names given indiscriminately to the character who personifies man's mortal part. But in Chapter III and the two final chapters, Natural Man again stands for the whole creature. In this second part of the *Dialogue* the Soul, with its imperfections, is opposed to the pure Spirit and holds colloquies with it.

Most of beautiful Part III is given up to converse of the Soul with her Lord, the author distinguishing in Chapters IV and X between Soul and Spirit as she does in Part II. In Chapter XI she seems, consistently enough, to identify the spirit and the "naked" soul. In Chapter IX she pauses in her skyey flights, and having come to earth uses Natural Man in the same sense as creature.

It should be remembered that this inspired, vehement, warm-hearted nun was no scholar. Her work reads as though she poured out what she had to say on paper, not staying to choose words, not revising or hardly revising. If she is sometimes careless of exactitude, she compensates for it by spontaneity. Like Saint Catherine in the *Treatise on Purgatory* she is conscious that her meaning is at times too deep and high for full expression. "To use them (words)", she says, "is like writing with black and ill smelling ink; yet by this means or some other many notions are understood which would not otherwise be known." The notions she would impart are indeed always discernible.

PART I

CHAPTER I

*How the Soul and the Body propose to keep company and
how they take Self-love to make a third with them.*

I saw (said she) a Soul and a Body talking together.
The Soul spoke first.

SOUL: O my Body, God has created me for love
and for delight; I would therefore turn to some place
where I can fulfil my purpose, and I would have thee
come with me peaceably, for thou too wilt get good
from this. We will go through the world. If I find
something which pleases me I will enjoy it. Thou wilt
do likewise when thou findest what pleases thee; each
of us will enjoy the best he finds.

BODY: Though I am obliged to do what pleases thee,
I see that thou, none the less, canst not work all thy
will without me. If then it be thy will that we go, let
us first come to an understanding so that we may not
dispute by the way. I am well content with what thou
hast said. But each of us most patiently let his companion
enjoy in peace whatever good he may find. Thus peace
will be kept between us and we shall bear with each
other. I say this because I would not have thee betray
me when I have met with some pleasant thing, saying,
"I do not wish to stay here so long; I would go else-
where on my own business." If I had then to give up
my purpose so as to follow thy will, I declare that it
would be the death of me and thus our plan would come

to nought. Lest this happen, it seems well to me that we take another with us, a just person, owning nothing apart from us, and that we submit all our differences to him.

SOUL: I am well content. But who shall this third be?

BODY: It shall be Self-love, who dwells with us both. He will give me my due and I shall enjoy it with him; he will do as much for thee, giving thee what thou needest. In this way each of us will fulfil his purpose as befits his degree.

SOUL: And if we find food pleasing to both of us, what shall we do?

BODY: Then that one of us who can will eat more than the other, so long as there be enough for us both. Thus we shall have no disputes. And if there be not enough, Self-love shall give to each of us his share. But it would be strange to find food agreeable to two whose tastes are contrary, unless the taste of one or other of us were changed, and that by nature could not be.

SOUL: By nature I am mightier than thou, so I have no fear that thou wilt convert me to thy tastes.

BODY: And I am in my own home where I have many, many things to enjoy with which I can delight myself. So thou wilt not be able to convert me to thy tastes, for all that thou art stronger than I. Rather would I, being as I have said at home, convert thee to mine, the more because I wish to love and delight thee. For thou goest out to seek things thou dost not see nor taste nor understand, nor dost thou know what to make of them.

SOUL: Let us try then; but let us first set up some order so that we may stay at peace with each other. Let each of us have his week; during mine I would have thee do what pleases me, even as, when thy week comes, I will do all thou wilt, saving always, for as long as I live, any offence against our Creator. But if I come to die, if, that is, thou shouldst lead me into sin, then from that moment I shall fulfil all thy commands, as thy servant; I shall be converted to thy will and delight in what delights thee. When we are thus joined together, none other than God can ever put us asunder, for so to do would be against free will. Thus in this world and the next we shall taste together all good and evil that may come to us. And it will be the same for thee if I am able to conquer thee. Look, here comes Self-love. I know, Self-love, that thou hast heard all we have said. Wilt thou make a third with us, be our judge and our companion on our journey?

SELF-LOVE: I am content for I feel that I shall be very well off with you. To each of you I will give his due: that can do me no harm. I shall live with the one of you as with the other, and if one of you do me violence so that I have not wherewith to live, I shall at once withdraw with the other, for not for anything do I mean to lack food.

BODY: Surely I will never forsake thee.

SOUL: Nor will I, for we are all of one mind, and understand, above all, that offence against God is an excepted thing, and that the one of us who sins will always have the other two against him. Now, in the Lord's name, let us set out, and as my rank is highest the first week will be mine.

BODY: I am content. Lead me on and do with me what is reasonable. Here is Self-love who consents as I do.

Then the Soul said within herself:

CHAPTER II

How the Soul and the Body begin each to have his week, in which each, in turn, refreshes himself according to his pleasure and taste.

SOUL: I who am pure and unstained by sin will begin by considering my first creation and all the other benefits I have received from God. I was created for great

beatitude and so high in rank that almost I am above
the choirs of angels; I see in myself a mind all but
divine; I feel myself ever drawn by my pure mind to
meditate on divine things and contemplate them;
ever I long to eat the bread of the angels. I am truly
invisible, and therefore I would feed only on things
invisible and delight in them only; for this was I made
and therein I find rest. I know no other need than to
fortify myself here above the heavens and put all else
beneath my feet. All this week, therefore, I would stay
in contemplation; nothing else do I hold of any account.
Let him who can feed himself where I do, be fed; let
him who cannot have patience. But I see that my companions are out of temper. I will go to them. Well,
comrades, I have finished my week. Thou, Body,
shalt treat me as thou wilt in thine. But tell me how
you have fared during mine?

SELF-LOVE: We have fared ill, since neither Self-love
nor mortal Body can enter the regions where thou
hast been. We have had not the least nourishment
and have been as though dead. But we hope for our
revenge.

BODY: This week is mine. Come with me, Soul,
for I would shew thee what great things God has made
for me. Look; admire the sky and the earth with all
their adornments, the sea with its fish, the air with its
birds, all the kingdoms and lordships and towns and pro-
vinces with their spiritual and temporal endowments,
the great worth of their many treasures, their songs
and melodies, and their meats of all kinds to feed me.
All these I will never lack while I am in the world. See
many other pleasures which I can enjoy, without offend-
ing God since He created them all for me. Thou hast
not shewn me thy country as I shew thee mine. And
because I cannot fulfil my purpose unless thou deignest
to grant that I enjoy it, I will remind thee how much
thou art bound to me. Think no longer of going off to
that country of thine and leaving me here on earth

without food. Thou canst not do it for it would kill me, and so thou wouldst be the cause of my death and wouldst offend God. Moreover, we would both be against thee. I have the advantage over thee that I can enjoy all these things while I live, and afterwards, in the next life, enjoy thy country too, if I save myself with thee as I wish to do. Know that it concerns me that thou shouldst save thyself for I must ever be with thee. Think not that I seek anything against reason or against God. Enquire of Self-love, our companion, if I speak truth. I ask not for what is unjust; I will abide by his judgment. I am sure that even in God's sight I could not do with less than what I seek of thee.

CHAPTER III

How Self-love blames the Soul and the Body and how he would settle their differences. How the Soul thereupon laments. How the Body agrees with Self-love and claims what he needs.

SELF-LOVE: I have seen what moves you both on this journey and I should find you reasonable if both of you had not passed, in the order of charity, all bounds, for God has said, "Love thy neighbour as thyself". First, for the Soul: she took no account whatever of us, so that almost we were in danger of death. Then I saw the Body shew the Soul many things, more indeed than will be needed. Thou, O Soul, must curb thy eagerness and bend to the needs of thy neighbour, that is of the Body, and to my needs too who have come to live with you. I found nothing for me in that country of thine; it is a place where less than anywhere can I dwell. And thou, Body, let what thou needest suffice thee, for anything more would be harmful to thee and to the Soul if she allowed it thee. But if thou seekest only what thou needest, each of you will live moderately, as befits his degree, and I shall be able to stay with you both. Thus united, each of us will enjoy the other's goods discreetly. If thou wouldst use thy Body, O Soul, thou must give him what he needs, or he will die. If thou givest him what he needs, he will be quiet and thou wilt do with him what thou wilt, and thus you will be at peace and I shall dwell with the two of you. But unless thou dost as I say, I must go away, for I cannot live in your company. This is my opinion.

SOUL: I am very ill content and unwilling to have to stoop to the Body in so many things, and I fear that if with this show of necessity, he thus satisfies himself, the two of you will make me delight in what delights him, and so I shall lose the more for the less. I fear that you will give me, who see you so famished, so much to do that you will change me from spiritual to earthly, for as I taste earthly things I shall lose my taste for what is spiritual. And I fear too that my understanding will be darkened and my will defiled. Help me, O my God!

BODY: It seems to me that Self-love has said all there is to be said and that we can be happy in his company. As for thee, Soul, thou mayst believe that if the things God has created were harmful to souls, He would not have created them. The Soul has been created so mighty and worthy that she can be hindered only by her own will, which is so respected by God that He never forces it. Therefore neither I nor anyone else can have aught of thee but what thou willest, as and when it pleases thee. Thou holdest the reins in thy hand; give to each what he needs and let who will cry for the rest.

SOUL: What then are these necessaries that thou mayst not lack? Name them to me: I would provide them so that I no longer have to think of them, for even to think of them is a great travail to me.

BODY: I need raiment, food, drink, sleep, service and something in which to take delight. And tire me not if thou wouldst attend to the spirit. If I were starving I could not be attentive to thy words. But if thou wilt stoop to my needs, thou wilt be able to collect thy mind and to think that if God has made so many things delightful to this mortal Body, He must have made still more and greater things for thee, O Soul immortal. Thus God will be ever praised and each of us will be fed as befits his degree. If some dispute arise between us, it will be settled by our Self-love here, who is very cunning, and he will be able to live with us and we with him in very holy peace.

SOUL: Well then, I will provide for your needs, being unable to do other, but I fear that you are already leagued against me. What you say seems so just that I am bound to yield to it, although I suspect you as I hear you speaking so much of what I should do and saying so often that you can do nothing without me. But perhaps, with God's help, I shall one day get myself out of your hands, and then I shall live without you and for His honour.

CHAPTER IV

The Soul, the Body and Self-love pursue their journey.
The Soul can no longer have her whole week for the Body lengthens his. The Soul lets herself be persuaded by Self-love, with a show of the Body's needs and his own. The Soul laments and proposes to give up her week.

BODY: Let us then go straight on with our journey, passing through the world in agreement. Each shall attend to his own business, seeking the food and the delights meet for his degree.

SOUL: Once more I have my week. But alas, I cannot do with it what I did with my first! Each of them drags me down, putting forward his needs for which I have to provide. Thus I spend my time, of which barely half is left me, bearing with my companions as best I can. Great reluctance weighs me down like a burden, as I leave so great a thing as divine contemplation to get food for beasts. The difference between this week and the other one I had is like that between black and white.

BODY: Now comes my week. I feel starved by the fasts the Soul has put on me, although nowadays, I see, she supplies my needs. So now, in this week, I will feed well and get strong. Already I am much fatter, and I am not afraid the Soul will harm me in her week, for she can no longer keep up to the height of her first, but stoops to my needs and those of Self-love. Every day we get on, and we gain on her so much that I have my week and the half of hers. For my needs are more every day and she cannot resist them.

SOUL: O Self-love, I see now that my arguments for going my own way were stolen from me so that I might stoop to thy many needs and those of the Body. I fear to pass all bounds as I let myself be guided by you who are so full of yourselves; I fear that in the end it will fare ill with us all. But tell me truly, thou who art our mediator, how does the thing seem to thee?

SELF-LOVE: Soul, thou didst set thyself for no reason at such a distance from us, and didst raise thyself to such a height, that it seems to thee now a great matter to give way to another's needs. Little by little thou wilt get thyself in order and our company will no longer seem as irksome to thee as now it does. Fear nothing; God will provide. Wholly blessed in this world thou canst not be; thy beatitude will be in the next life. Take now what thou canst have and do the best thou canst.

SOUL: I see I cannot defend myself against you who are in your own home and joined together against me. It is vain for me to have my week, for you leave me not one quiet day, with your continual needs for which you take more of my time than is left me for myself. Then when your turn comes, you want all your week, without any hindrance, saying it is all yours. In the end, I cannot but come off badly. I have it in mind no longer to have a week. Let each seek his own livelihood and feed where he can. I will try to bear with you as best I can, since I cannot do otherwise.

BODY AND SELF-LOVE: We, too, think this will be well. Thus each of us can live in peace and keep within his limits, all the more since thou, Soul, hast seen thy error.

CHAPTER V

The Soul lets herself be drawn to the delights of the Body and of Self-love and falls into the pit of sin. How little contentment the Soul gets from earthly things and how little the Body needs to be satisfied. Of the anguish of the Soul.

And going thus through the world, one wanted one thing and one another, and each fed in his own way. The Soul went with her eyes on the domain of the Body and allowed him many things he said he needed. But the Body's appetites, which were joined to Self-love, grew day by day, and Self-love bound them strongly together so that they might not be sundered. It all seemed reasonable and necessary to the Body and Self-love who wished never to lack anything; moreover, if the Soul did not yield them daily some new thing to feed them afresh, they grumbled, saying they were wronged. Thus the Soul was led into an infinite and immeasurable ocean of love for earthly things and delight in them, all of which things joined together to change her until she, no more than the Body or Self-love, ever spoke or thought except as these companions of hers desired. When she would have attended to her own business, the disorderly appetites of her companions so went counter to her that she dared not speak. Then she said, in her unhappiness: "If these two lead me as far into their country as I led them into mine in my first

week, who then can save me from their hands? They
will indeed work their will on me, pleading necessity."

Now this Soul, who wanted some food or other on
which to live, lest she fell into melancholy (having been
created for love and happiness), began to let herself
be driven before the wind, even though she were blown
out of her course. Since she could no longer live in
her own country, she fed by that wayside on what she
found, saying, to make the thing seem good, "These
beauties, pleasures, boons, delights and grandeurs,
and all the adornment of created things, are means by
which to know and taste things divine"; and while she
enjoyed them, she said, "O how good and beautiful
the things of Heaven must be!" Travelling thus with
her companions, day by day she lost, more and more,
the divine instinct natural to her, and satisfied herself
with the food of swine and other beasts, as the Body did;
so that after a short while the three companions were
in great unity.

Since they were thus united, in great amity and
peace, never gainsaying each other, I leave you to think
how the order of higher reason fared. None spoke of it
now. They sought only the things of the earth; their
tastes, loves and pleasures were all earthly; spiritual
things seemed bitter to these travellers; fearing their
earthly tastes might be disturbed, they neither spoke
of them nor could bear to hear a word of them. The
journey went on in this way for a very long time. Only
a slight prick of remorse still lingered in the Soul and
she took very little account of it, albeit at times she paid
it more attention than at others, when the risk of losing
everything altogether by death came back to her mind.
Then she would feel a great fear, but when this moment
had passed she went on as before. There was only
one difference between the companions: while they
all tried, with all their powers, to satisfy their appetites,
they could not all do it, for the Soul, who was one of
them, had an infinite capacity and all earthly things

were finite. The Soul could find neither satisfaction
nor rest; the more she sought rest, the less she found
it, for every day she went further from God in whom
was her true rest.

These earthly things so blinded this Soul that she
believed she would find rest on earth, and therefore
she studied only what she could do to be satisfied, and
when something did not satisfy but even disgusted her,
her inward blindness led her to put hope in something
else. Passing thus from one thing to another she forgot
herself, and going from hope to hope wasted time,
but by the Lord God's merciful ordinance she never
fulfilled her intent. For if man could find rest on earth,
then surely few souls would be saved, for in the midst
of earthly things they would be so changed that they
would never seek to escape from them.

By a natural instinct a soul aspires to delight. Blinded
by the body, it seeks delight only through the body,
which leads it from one thing to another that they may
feed together. But the soul, having a capacity for infinite
things, cannot through the body find aught to quiet it;
like a senseless thing it lets itself be led by the body,
yet is never satisfied.

As for the body, the more it has turned the soul to its
own ends, the more means of joy and satisfaction in
earthly things it has, only because the soul has yielded
to it. The body would be without taste or delight if
the soul did not yield to it. Since the body is knit with
the soul, for which the things of the earth are not enough,
and since moreover the body can neither follow the
soul nor give it the joy and delight it would have, therefore the soul is starved by the body. This happens
because the body has appetites which can be satisfied.
When it has what it needs, whatever that may be, it
loses taste for the thing and takes no more delight in
it. Though indeed it still has the desire to seek new
things and satisfy natural appetites, for the body can
find nothing to satisfy it wholly, not because the soul

fails to stoop to its needs, nor because ill-health is a hindrance, but because there is an end to its capacity. Thus it is that the body and the soul are in pain together.

It was matter for anguish to this Soul to see herself in a vessel which held so little, which a little food contented, and in which, out of respect for this Body, she must stay though she died of hunger (being kept from satisfying her natural instinct for delight). Before the Body had satisfied his appetite, it had seemed that all things created would not be enough for him; and the Soul would have fed by means of the Body because she had an instinct to do what he would. But she saw what a little thing satisfied him, and that, having lost his taste, he could not get it back and was in torment because he could not enjoy the things set before him, and that the more he forced his taste the less he had of it. Indeed, if a man did himself violence to recover his taste, he would risk death.

When the Soul saw this, she spoke to Self-love, saying:

CHAPTER VI

How the Soul, wishing to go on differently, holds new converse with Self-love. Of the nature of Self-love. Of the little the Body needs to satisfy him as compared with his desires. How the Soul falls into the pit of misery and despair.

SOUL: O Self-love, seest thou that thou and I are both in pain and ill fed? You two have made me stoop so low to satisfy your appetites that I fare very ill. I am no longer fed in Heaven and you cause me to die of hunger on earth. How does this journey seem to thee?

SELF-LOVE: I see that you are both ill content, hitherto with reason. But let us still go on; it may be that by the way we shall find food fit for us all. I have learnt by experience that this Body is a small eater, but as for me, I cannot find as much food as I want, for in one instant I eat what would be enough for the Body for a year. How then can it fare with thee, whose capacity is greater, beyond compare, than mine? This is what we will do: we will continue our journey, seeking as we go for food more fit for us than what we have come upon hitherto, and when we find it we will give the Body what he needs, and compared to us he needs little. After that, let him squeal for more!

SOUL: What meats do you eat? And what food can we find to content us both and to feed the Body too?

SELF-LOVE: My appetite is a good one: I feed both on earthly and on spiritual meats, and if but thou leadest me not where thou wast for thy first week, I shall find food anywhere else. So long as I get a living while I keep company with someone, I may be said never to forsake him; I gather so much that my companions are never left in need; rather I enrich them.

SOUL: I know that on earth we could never have the food which would content us both for it is not plentiful enough there to satisfy me, and as for Heaven (where it abounds), I have come so far thence that I no longer know nor can find the way thither. I see that God shut the gates of His grace on us in that instant in which we decided to feed ourselves on the pleasures of this world, and that He has let us run after our appetites. Now that we are in confusion and despair in our chosen pasturages, we would return to Him, but for our own profit and not out of that true and pure charity which the Lord asks of us and by which He ever works in us.

When I think how much I have done for you and how much I have justly lost, I know I deserve to be abhorred by God and you and the world and hell. I am confounded almost to despair, perceiving that you have led me back to earthly things, in which I thought to find something for your needs and my own while we had to be together in this world. But now, having tried all things, I believe that none of us could be quieted or satisfied even if we had all the good we could ask for on the earth. All your appetites too I have seen and have tried; I have seen you on fire with your desire to try them out by your senses, but they have been soon satisfied and you have been at a loss because of the little pleasure you have received from what you had so eagerly desired. But though at a loss you were not in despair, for you still hoped in the future, and still, again and again, you were left as you had been before. When your appetites had been assuaged I was starving, and when I would have returned to my country, following my instinct, I no longer found the means to which I was used, for I had gone far from my first path which was pure, straight and clear and lent itself to all spiritual works. I had yielded to some disorders of this Body, who pleaded his needs, and after his needs he claimed more than he needed. Soon I found myself wrapped and bound in sin; I lost grace and grew blind and heavy; I who had been spiritual came to be all of earth. Now, wretch that I am, I can no longer move except downwards to the earth, which drags me to every evil thing. For I am an outcast from my country who let myself be dragged by you, Body and Self-love, whither it pleases you to take me. You have brought me so far that I no longer gainsay your appetites.

Little by little you have so converted, or rather perverted me that I feed on all that feeds you; we are so agreed and united that blindly I desire whatever you desire. Almost have I, a spiritual soul, become an earthly body. And thou, Self-love, hast chained us to thyself so strongly and holdest us in so inseparable an embrace, that I, poor wretch, am blind and smothered and as dead to spiritual things. All but blind as I am to the light, taking pleasure in earthly and bodily things, no good is left in me saving an inward remorse which gives me little rest. Yet I forget myself as best I can among these things of the earth on which I feed; I go among them; I waste my time on them; day by day they gain on me more and more; and the more I depart from God the unhappier I am to have wandered far from the good natural to me, which is God.

Such were the reasons this wretched Soul gave for her many sighs, yet she knew not their cause. This was God's instinct, which she had naturally; for God, who is all good, never forsakes His creature utterly in this life but often gives him some inspiration. Thus man is helped if he will, but if he refuse the help his state is often worsened by the ingratitude he has shewn for the grace vouchsafed him.

This mean Soul soon found herself with such a burden of sin and ingratitude on her back that, seeing no way of ridding herself thereof, she had no hope of escaping from her state. It came about that she not only took pleasure in sin but even boasted of it. The more grace she had received, the greater was her blindness and her despair of returning to God. It was impossible for her to be delivered from her plight by human means; God alone, of His infinite mercy and grace, could rescue her. As for her, she wanted only earthly things; her tastes, her love, her intentions, her joy were fixed on the things of the earth. Everything else she hated; even to speak of anything else disgusted her; what had once seemed to her sweet she now found most bitter. She had exchanged the taste for Heaven for the taste for the earth.

CHAPTER VII

Of the light by which God made the Soul see all her faults and the state to which she had come. Of her resignation, confidence and conversion.

God in His goodness let this Soul stray for a while among the things of this world, and many things befell her which caused her deep disgust; far from satisfying her they wearied her ever more. Then this merciful God sent her a light which opened up her understanding and shewed her all her errors and the danger in which she stood, from which God alone could deliver her. Seeing whither she had come and the path she followed, and knowing that its end would be bodily death on the one hand and the death of the soul on the other, and that she was in the midst of many enemies and was suffering herself to be led like a beast to the slaughter, and even seemed to be going there merrily, she was shocked in all her being, and turning wholly to God, as well as she knew how, she said with a great and lamentable sigh:

"O wretch that I am! Who will ever deliver me from all this woe? God alone can deliver me. *Domine fac ut videam lumen* that I may escape from these many snares!"

Having thus turned to God and asked for His help (for she knew that without it she could no longer move save to go from bad to worse), the Soul in that instant put her trust wholly in Him, and then let Him work as He would and as much as He would. And she said further:

"Henceforth I would take from the benign hand of God whatever may come to me, but not sin, for my sins are my own and when I commit them I go against the divine will. In sin there is self, and wherever self is there is wilful sin."

This first resolve was made to God by the Soul secretly and in the spirit, without any outward sign.

Now when God sees that man mistrusts himself and gives himself up to hope in His providence, from which he awaits all the good he can have, then He swiftly stretches out His holy hand to provide for him. God stays always by our side and knocks, and if the door be opened He enters, and little by little drives away all His enemies and brings the soul back to the first innocence in which He created it. God does this by divers means, ways and states, as He sees He can best work on the creature.

Now we will speak of His work, wrought of His pure love, and of how He cleansed a soul from self-love.

CHAPTER VIII

*Of many lights which the Soul received and of the pure
love of God. Of the remorse He sends us.*

First, when God would purge a soul of self-love, He sends
His divine light, shewing it a spark of the pure love He
bears us, and the great things which by this love, having
no need of us even for the least thing, He works and has
worked in us. For we are His enemies because of our many
offences against Him, and by our nature we are apt
only for illdoing and quick to offend Him.

He also shewed this Soul of which I speak that our
faults can never so anger Him that He will cease His
benefits to us while we are in this world. Nay, rather
it seems that the further our sins take us from Him,
the more He calls us, with many pricks and divers
inspirations, so that we may not utterly depart from His
love but that He may ever love us and do us good.
The better for this end, He uses many, many means and
follows very many paths. A soul attentive to what He
does cries out in admiration, "What am I that God
verily seems to care only for me?"

And among other things God revealed to this Soul
the pure love with which He created us, asking only that
we give Him back this same love and stay with Him
for ever, and expecting nothing in return save union
with us.

And the Soul was made to see that this love of God
was shewn forth chiefly in the creation of the pure angels,
and then in that of the creature, Father Adam, created
out of the purity and truth of the love with which God
Himself would be loved and obeyed. If God had subjected our Father Adam and his descendants to nothing
after He had made him so excellent, each man, looking

on the excellence of his soul and body and his empire over all created things, would have thought himself God. Yet God subjected Adam only a very little, that he might still know his Maker and be obedient to Him.

And God made this Soul see that He had created man for a greater good, which was that at last he might be borne away, soul and body, to his heavenly country.

Then God shewed her the calamity which had overtaken her because of her sin, and that this calamity could be undone only by a new manifestation of love which God needs must make.

And He caused her to see the burning love which Our Lord Jesus Christ testified on earth in all that He did, from His incarnation to His ascension, to deliver us from eternal damnation. In one instant God, by His most pure working, shewed all these things to this Soul of which I speak.

Thereafter He made her see the liberty in which He created her, subjecting her to no creature but only to her Creator, and giving her a free will which could be constrained by none, neither on the earth while she stayed on it nor in Heaven.

He shewed her with what patience He had waited for her and borne with her many sins, which were such that had she died in them she would have been justly damned.

And He shewed her that she had often been in danger of death and that, of His pure love alone, He had delivered her so that in time she might know her error and escape eternal damnation.

Then God made her see the inspirations He had given her to snatch her from sin, and how, although she had not yielded to them but had in everything gone against His will, He mercifully had not ceased still to inspire her, now in one way and now in another, and had so cajoled her free will that, as it were, He had forced her to do what His goodness desired, with a care and patience not to be compared to any human love ever seen on earth,

God also shewed this Soul that the great love He bears man is never troubled by anger: always He loves him and seeks to be united to him by love; His instinct to love never fails, and therefore He never ceases to work towards union with us by His pure love which burns but does not consume. Only to sin is He horrible and dreadful, because the least imperfection cannot be where He is. He hates only sin which alone keeps His love from working in us, and were it not for the wretchedness and weight of sin the very demons would burn with divine love.

Moreover God made her see that His hand ever holds glowing rays of love to set the hearts of men on fire and pierce them, and that it is sin which goes against Him. Take sin away and all will be at peace; put sin back and all will be confusion.

She saw, too, that God's love for man, however great his sin, can never be so wholly quenched that it ceases to bear him up while he is in this life, but beyond this life there is hatred and eternal fury.

Yet she saw a ray of God's love shine even in hell. For the impious man deserves infinite pain in infinite time, but divine mercy has ordained for him infinity only of time, putting a limit to his pain. Thus God could justly condemn him to greater pain than He has given him.

This soul also saw a certain ray of love come forth from the divine spring and turn towards man as though it would make him nothing.[1] And she saw that when this ray was hindered, then, could God feel pain, His pain would be of the greatest there can be. All this ray had to do was to seek to pierce the soul, and if it failed only the soul was to blame. For to enter the soul the ray surrounds it on all sides, and yet a soul blinded by self-love perceives it not. And when God sees a soul working its own damnation, and cannot enter into it

[1] Here, of course, Battista, having in her mind the necessary self-annihilation, exaggerates since God could not annihilate a soul.

because of its obstinacy, then God seems to say: "The love I bear this soul is so great that I would never forsake it." But the soul bereft of divine love becomes almost as malignant as this love is sweet and good. Almost, I say, for God still has some mercy on it. This Soul of which I speak heard God say, "By My will I would never have thee damn thyself. So great is the love I bear thee that were it possible for Me to suffer in thy stead I would do it willingly, but since love cannot dwell where there is fault, I cannot but forsake thee. Through Me thou wouldst be fit for all blessedness, but forsaken by Me thou art fit for all evil." She also saw many other workings and works of love on souls, which were such as no tongue can tell.

It was this ray of love which struck this Soul of which I speak. In one instant she saw and felt a fire of love which had come from that divine source and by which she was all but rapt from herself, without understanding, speech or feeling, busied only with this pure and simple love as God had shewn it her. This sight nevermore left her mind; evermore she saw this pure love turned on her.

It was also shewn her how unknowing she had been of this love and how many were her faults, and in her faults she saw herself and all she was apt to do against this pure love. Then she was sunk in such contempt for herself that she would have told her sins publicly through the town, and with an interior cry she uttered these words (for she could not do other): "O Lord, no more of the world for me! No more sin!"

But for all this which she saw, her other vision of the love shed by the ray, of which I have told, did not fail her, so that her mind was still busied about that pure love, in which she perceived all other things, and especially those of which it behoved her to purge herself. Nor did she deem her sins grave because of the punishment they deserved but only because they offended the great goodness of God. For she saw how much God loved her, with most pure love which never left her heart, and from her heart turned ever back to God from whom it had come. This love it was which melted her, so that she could not but do all her works with the purity which was in her heart; and she stayed so united to that ray that nevermore could anything lower than God come between it and her—I mean anything which touched her affections.

CHAPTER IX

The Soul speaks to Self-love and the Body of the truth she has perceived, and tells them she would lose herself if she followed them. She threatens to do to them what they would have done to her, making them subject to her. Of their displeasure.

When the Soul had seen all that love had, with such clearness, purity and care, wrought in her, she stood still and said to the Body and Self-love:

SOUL: My brothers, I have seen the truth of the love of God with which He would work in me, and I no longer care about you nor make any account of your needs, far less of what you may say, for I know verily that by attending to you I would come to perdition. If I had not made trial of the thing I would not believe it. Pleading good and necessity, you have led me even to death by sin, and it is no fault of yours that I have not come to eternal damnation. Now I intend to do to you what you would have done to me. I shall regard you no more than I would my chief enemies. Think not that you will ever again come to an understanding with me; give up hope of that as though you were damned. I shall try to go back to that first path I followed, from which by your wiles you made me stray. I hope by means of the divine light not to be taken in by you again, but to manage our business so well that each of us will have what he needs. To satisfy your appetites you made me do what I should not have done; and to satisfy the spirit I will, in my turn, lead you whither you would not go. As for the damage you may suffer, though you should die of it I shall not trouble about it, any more than you troubled about me who gave myself up to you and let you work all your will on me. I hope to master your wills so that I shall raise you out of your natural way of being.

When the Body and Self-love saw that the Soul had so much light that they could no longer deceive her, they were very ill content and said:

BODY AND SELF-LOVE: O Soul, we are, saving justice, thy subjects; do with us what thou wilt. If we cannot live otherwise, we will live by plunder. Thou wilt do all thou canst against us and we will do all the evil we can against thee. In the end each of us will have his deserts.

SOUL: One thing I will tell you for your comfort. It is this: while we journey as I have said you will seem unhappy. But when I have taken away your superfluity (albeit the thing will surely give you much pain) you will be content with all I have said and done, and will be eternal sharers with me of my wellbeing. So dispose yourselves to patience, for at last we shall all taste divine peace. Now I will allow you only what you need; later you shall have all you desire. I will bring you to sure and great satisfaction, so that you yourselves, even in this life, will not wish for anything more. Hitherto you have, as you yourselves know, found no sort of satisfaction whatever things you may have enjoyed, and you have tried all things. Now I hope to lead you to a place of great and unending contentment, which will begin and will grow little by little, 'in suchwise that at last the Soul's peace, which will be communicated to the Body, will be enough to sweeten not one but a thousand hells. Before I can bring you thither there will be much to do, but I hope that (by God's light and help) we will all get there, safe and sound. Let this be enough for your comfort; henceforth I shall not speak but do.

BODY: I see thee so terrible and so resolute to get me down that I fear thou mayst run into some excess for which we shall both be the worse. I will therefore remind thee of divers things and make thee a few petitions, after which I shall let thee do as thou wilt. Remember that after the love of God comes the love of thy neighbour, which should, in bodily things, begin with thine own Body. Thou art bound to keep thy Body not only in life but also in health; no less canst thou do if thou wouldst succeed in what thou hast resolved. As to life: I tell thee I am necessary to thee for when I am dead thou wilt have neither the means to increase thy glory nor the time to cleanse thyself of all thy imperfections as thou desirest, but wilt pass through Purgatory, which will seem to thee a far harder penance than to keep a body in this world. As to health: when the body is healthy, the soul's powers and the body's senses are more apt to receive divine light and inspiration, even with a feeling of pleasure which is communicated by the soul to the body; but if I am sick then thou wilt lack these things, with many others which I pass over for fear of saying too much. I have told thee what seems to me to the purpose for me and thee, so that each of us may have his due and we may reach the haven of salvation without reproach either in Heaven or on earth.

SOUL: I am taught all that I need to know inwardly by divine light, and outwardly by the arguments thou hast put forward and many others which can be guessed. Henceforward, however, I would be quit of outward arguments and persuasions and regard only those which are higher, and are so well ordered that they are just to all. To each they give what he needs so that none can complain saving by his own fault, for he who complains shews that he is not yet in good order and has not submitted his appetites to higher reason. Let me alone,

O Body; I shall so do that thou thyself wilt change thy way of thinking, and live in a contentment so great that thou wouldst not believe in it if thou didst not try it.

Once I was mistress, when at first I would have attended to the spirit; afterwards, by cheating me, thou madest thyself my brother, and we agreed together with Self-love lest one of us might overbear the other. But little by little you two came so to lead me that I found myself your slave and could do only what you would. Now I will again be mistress, and I make this bargain with thee. If thou wilt serve me as a servant, I shall be content and will let thee lack nothing a servant needs. But if thou wilt not, I will force thee to serve me as a slave, and so ill shalt thou be treated that thou wilt wish to serve me for love. All disputes will end thus for I intend, by one means or another, to be served and still to be mistress.

CHAPTER X

Of the vision the Soul received of the goodness and providence of God, and of the faults and sins that were in her. How she considered herself and of her hatred for Natural Man.

And thus this enlightened Soul began to see all her faults, the disorder in which she had been and the dangers into which she and the Body had run unknowingly, and she saw that her backsliding would not have been stayed without God's providence. And considering God's goodness to man, sunk in so many sins, she was amazed and astonished. For when a man begins to see God's goodness and providence, then God shews that man all the faults He would remedy, and in one instant the soul sees them in that divine light which is full of love. The Soul of which I speak, having had these two sure, true and clear visions (of God's goodness in providing for her out of pure love, and of herself sunk in sin and willingly going against God's infinite mercy), was brought up short and said:

SOUL: O Lord, I would never again offend Thee nor do anything contrary to Thy goodness, for this great goodness has filled me with confusion, and bound me to Thee so closely that I have resolved never again to depart from Thy ordinance, though it cost me a thousand bodily lives.

Then the Soul turned to herself and saw again her faults and evil instincts, and she said:

SOUL: Dost thou think thee well adorned now to meet thy Lord? How dost thou stand? Who will ever deliver thee from such wretchedness? Now thou seest how hideous and defiled thou art, who didst think thyself so fair and good. This has come to thee because thou hadst withdrawn into thyself with so much self-love that thou knewest no other paradise than to pursue sensuality. Now thou seest what all those things are before God; verily they are nothing else than the works of the devil and hell.

Then the Soul turned to Natural Man, and with a deep and piercing hatred said to him:

SOUL: I warn thee, O Natural Man, that if henceforth thou tellest me of this thing or that one that it is unfitting, I will put on thee things very fit for thee to bear. I will pay no more regard to thee than if thou wert a demon, for thy works have always been of the devil; so they will ever be and such only canst thou do. And since, like me, thou seest how grievous it is to offend God, I know not how thou wilt ever again be bold enough to think and speak of things meet to satisfy thy appetite, for thou knowest that ever thou goest against God's will. But I shall beware of thee as of the devil; and if thou cheatest me as the devil does, I shall put on thee such a penance as thou wilt remember another time.

Natural Man, having heard these words of the Soul, answered nothing, but like a guilty man led to judgment abased himself.

CHAPTER XI

*How the Soul, turning to God, acknowledged her own vileness.
How she was shewn what she would have been if she had
continued on her way. Of her lamenting and almost her
despair because of her offences, and of the confidence Our
Lord gave her by appearing to her in the spirit. Of the
wound she received.*

The Soul then turned her eyes to God, and having
that pure vision said:

SOUL: O Lord, what moved Thee to give such light
to this blind and filthy Soul, Thy enemy, who fled from
Thee and walked in ways contrary to Thy will, feeding
ever on sensual things, who would not be delivered
from her very evil state and therefore ever shunned all
that could take her out of it? As I think on myself,
I am amazed for I see that I am a most vile creature.

Then this Soul was shewn where she was, whither she
was bound, and what she would have carried with her
had she pursued that road. All these things she saw in
one instant, as they were and as they would have been
had God not provided. And seeing them, she was like
one half dead, so moved by fear and passion that she
seemed beside herself, and could but weep and sigh and
groan inwardly, saying:

SOUL: O wretch that I am, and wretched I would
have been had I continued on that road! What pain,
what travail I was ever forging for myself in this world,
and in the other I would have found myself God's enemy
and condemned to hell for all eternity!

For some time the Soul had this vision, which caused
her such deep pain that she could think of nothing else
nor shew any cheer. Sunk in melancholy, she knew
not what to do with herself, finding no resting-place,
neither in Heaven, for which she was not fit, nor on

earth, for she saw she deserved that the earth should swallow her. And it seemed to her that she ought neither to appear before men nor to consider in any way her own convenience or inconvenience. Acknowledging that she alone had done all the evil, she would have made satisfaction alone, without help from any other; and she said:

SOUL: I see it, my place is in hell, but only through death can I take that place. Alas, my God, what shall I do with myself? I know not where to hide; I go my way moaning; I find no place for me, for soiled as I am I dare not appear before Thee and yet I find Thee everywhere; and thus I am unbearable to myself. What then shall I do with this ugly and stained garment in which I am clothed? To weep avails me not; to sigh is no help to me; my contrition has not been accepted; and my penances bear no fruit, for they cannot make satisfaction for the pains I deserve unless God have pity on me and help me.

It seemed to the Soul who thus all but despaired that she could not make satisfaction nor have recourse to God's mercy; in herself she found nothing to give her confidence, yet was unwilling utterly to despair; she was in torment, bowed down by a weight of despair and acknowledging the gravity of her wrong-doing. Her heart laboured in great torment; inwardly she was in tears yet could not weep; she sighed in secret; her life was being burnt away, for she could neither speak nor eat nor sleep nor smile nor look up to Heaven; she had no taste left, neither spiritual nor bodily; she knew not where she was, whether in Heaven or on earth; she was like one insensate or amazed and beside herself. Willingly would she have hidden, so that none might find her and she might not be in another's company.

This Soul was so bewildered and so sunk in her knowledge of her offences against God that she was more like a frightened wild beast than a reasonable creature. This came of the clear vision given her of the gravity of her offences and the great harm they had wrought; if she had kept it in sight too long, her body would have been consumed even though it had been of diamond. But God, when He had left the vision with her until it was well imprinted on her, so that she could never forget it, provided for her as shall be told.

When one day she was in her home, Our Lord Jesus Christ appeared to her interior sight. He was covered with blood from head to foot, so that wherever He went blood seemed to rain on all the earth from His body. In secret, these words were spoken to the Soul: SEEST THOU THIS BLOOD? IT WAS ALL SHED FOR LOVE OF THEE AND FOR THE SATISFACTION OF THY SINS. These words wounded her with a great wound of love for Our Lord Jesus Christ, and gave her such confidence that her other and despairing vision was dispelled, and she took a little joy in Our Lord.

CHAPTER XII

Of another vision by which God shewed the Soul the love with which He had suffered for her. How she saw the wickedness of man and the benignity of the pure love of God. Of her offer of herself to God, and of the wound she received from the five springs of Jesus. Of His acceptance and His jealous care.

Another vision, greater than the first, was granted her, so great indeed that tongue could not tell nor mind imagine it. It was that God shewed her the love with which He had suffered for her. And when the Soul saw the pure and strong love which God bore her, she was so deeply wounded that she felt scorn for all other love and for every other thing which had come between her and God, that is for all saving God alone. Seeing this love, she saw also man's wickedness and how benign is God's pure love, and these two visions never again left her memory; the one of them brought back the other. But if she had seen the infinity of the goodness of God and all that, with so much pure love, it works for man (only a little of it had been shewn her), she would have swooned at such sweetness.

It was her sight of this love which made her see also the great wickedness of man, to benefit whom God's love ever works, as it were in spite of him, neither regarding the evil in him, nor ceasing (so benign is God) to work in him for his profit in infinite ways, not angered by his offences but rather working with pure love for their correction, ever attentive to man's profit. For this Soul, turning back to herself, saw her own wickedness, who had gone against God's great goodness, and so she began to see what is this being, man, almost as malignant and evil as God is good. And she was left in such despair of herself that never again could she see anything which was of man saving as one sees the devil in all his malignity, and if God had not tempered this vision the Soul and the Body would have swooned, as when she had had her other vision of divine love for man. Thus she despaired of herself, fearing she was past correction, nor would she lose more time in thinking how to correct herself, but put her trust in God's love only, and said to Him:

SOUL: Lord, I make Thee a present of myself, who no longer know what to do but know that I am fitted to make a hell of myself alone. I would exchange with Thee: I give this evil self into Thy hands, for Thou alone canst hide it in Thy goodness and so rule me that nothing proper to me be seen any more. Grant me, in return, to be filled with Thy pure love which quenches in me all other love; make me bring all to nothing in Thee; keep me so busied over Thee that there be neither time nor place for aught else to dwell with me.

Her most sweet Saviour answered that He was content, and at that very instant this part of her memory was taken from her. Then a ray of love was shed on her heart, and it was so burning and piercing and so wounded her inmost part that it took away from her, in one instant, all her loves, appetites, delights and whatsoever else was her own, all which she had ever had or could have in this world. She was left stript of all things, consenting in so far as she could to the work of love shewn her, which love drew her so that she was amazed, engrossed, changed and taken out of herself. She wept and sighed more, beyond compare, than when she had had her vision of her own wickedness.

This ray of love left an imprint on her by means of those five springs of Christ whence flow drops of burning blood, on fire with love for man. God granted her to know without pain what man is; she had the two visions, of God's love and of herself, at one time, as far as she could bear to see these things and live, and the sight of herself gave her no pain because her most gentle God had taken from her all the suffering it had caused her, albeit she still clearly saw what she was and how the Lord upheld her. It was revealed to her too that if God had ever left her, she would have been apt to shew in all her works the wickedness of the devil incarnate, and even more, for she saw herself as the devil incarnate. Being, however, in God's hands, she knew herself in good hands and could have no fear.

But the sight which crucified and consumed her was that of this ardent love of God for man. She said human tongue could never tell the vehemence of the fire it lit in her. This love which God shewed her gave her an instinct jealously to reject all which displeased God, and to keep strict watch on all her faults, however slight. Not only on her faults. It opened her eyes to all the imperfections and useless habits she had ever had, and this gave her strength and firmness to get rid of useless habits, caring nothing for hindrances. She took Natural Man no more into account than if she had never had him, nor cared for the flesh, the world or the devil.

She saw that with this love she was stronger than anything that went against her and than all the demons, for she was joined to God who is the true strength of all who fear, love and serve Him; and she saw that nothing which was her own could harm her any longer, for all things belonging to herself were in God's hand and held by His goodness.

CHAPTER XIII

Of the instinct this Soul had to rid herself of all superfluous things, even those which seemed necessary. Of the instinct she had for prayer, and of her mortifications.

God also gave this Soul an instinct to despise what was of self, so that, as far as she herself was concerned, she cared for all the things there are under the sky no more than if they were not.

The love she felt gave her also the instinct to take from Natural Man not only superfluous food but also what seemed necessary food; she did as much with clothes and with all companions; this love drew her to loneliness of mind and body and reduced her to her own company. Moreover it gave her the instinct for prayer, so that she was on her naked knees six or seven hours together, against the will of Natural Man; and though this made her suffer, she neither heeded her pains nor refused because of them to serve and to be as the spirit drew her.

All these instincts were the work only of God; neither the will for them nor their object was the Soul's. God, who had taken her into His power, willed to rule what belonged to her and take from her the instincts which were of Natural Man and the world, and to this end He gave her contrary instincts. He ruled that she should not eat fruit, which by nature she found pleasant and much liked, or meat, or any other thing which seemed superfluous. It was as though He held in His hand the measure of what she should eat, and since He willed her to lose her taste for food, He made her have hepatic aloes or pounded agaric always at hand, and when it seemed to her that she liked some one thing better than another she secretly put a pinch of this very bitter powder in it before she ate it. Her eyes were ever cast to the ground; she never smiled; she recognized none who passed near her for she was so constantly busy inwardly that outward things were, so to speak, wiped out from her sight. Always she seemed unhappy and yet was most happy. She sought to do without sleep by putting things which pricked her in her bed, but do what she would God never took sleep away from her; she slept against her will.

When Natural Man saw this great vehemence of the spirit and learnt that he counted no more than if he were not, and could in no way remedy his plight, he was very ill content, yet dared utter no word. Seeing Christ, the Judge, angered with him, he was like a thief in prison who dares not speak because he knows the evil he has done and fears he may fare yet worse if he say a word. One only hope lingered in him, that which one has during heavy rain that the bad weather will not last long, and this faint hope kept him patient. But such was the spirit's fury that it pressed on him from many sides, so that, saving when he slept, he could in no way recover, and he became dry, arid and pale, like a piece of wood. Then one day the Spirit and Natural Man conversed as follows:

CHAPTER XIV

Of the colloquy of the Spirit and Natural Man. How Natural Man complains of the Spirit's vehemence which he thinks he will not be able to bear.

SPIRIT: Natural Man, how does this way of life seem to thee?

NATURAL MAN: O Spirit, thou hast entered on this life with such fury that I think it will be impossible to persevere therein. I look for death to come of it, or at least sickness, sooner perhaps than thou thinkest: thus thou wilt not win what thou seekest in this world, but wilt be forced to go to purgatory, and there wilt suffer more in one instant than thou wouldst in all the time we could spend in this world. I will be in the grave, which will be a less evil to me than thus to live. Thou wilt go into the fire and be worse off than I. Speak now in thy turn; I have no more to say.

SPIRIT: I look for neither death nor sickness; evil makes thee rave. All thy ill humours have been purged; abstinence has been healthy for thee; but I see that thou hast lost flesh and colour, and since the mill of divine love would soon grind thee all away, I know that it will work on emptiness unless I put grain into it, and thus all would be spoilt. I will so provide that each of us will be satisfied, neither dying nor falling sick.

And so great a light had indeed been shed on this Spirit that it saw even the least mote that was contrary to itself, and seeing it wiped it out. The Spirit did what it would with Natural Man, who withstood it not; so vigorous was the Spirit that Natural Man would have suffered yet more had he rebelled. When Natural Man saw himself in this plight, and that he could not hope for the least relief from the Spirit, he said to himself:

NATURAL MAN: If I were but fed at all by spiritual things and could content myself with what contents the Spirit, I would get comfort. Otherwise I know not what I shall do, nor how still to be patient in my great distress, or to bear the pains by which I am bound and imprisoned.

It happened that this creature, thinking thus, was in church, and when she had communicated a ray of light came to her and therewith a feeling, and it seemed to the Soul and Natural Man that they were in eternal life, as it is said *Cor meum et caro mea exultaverunt in Deum vivum*. So great were the savour and the divine light they enjoyed that even Natural Man was fed, and said:

NATURAL MAN: Thus I too can live.

But when this moment had passed, pure love began to cry out at what it saw and the Spirit said: "O Lord, Lord, I want no proofs from Thee; I seek no feelings; nay, I flee them all as I would demons, for they hinder pure love which should be naked. Man can attach himself to feelings by the spirit and the body, pleading that he seeks perfection. Therefore, Lord, I pray Thee nevermore to give me such things as these; they are not made for me or for any who would have divine love in nakedness."

CHAPTER XV

Natural Man complains that the Spirit does not keep its promise. The Spirit defends itself. Of the danger of spiritual tastes seemingly good. How they are more dangerous than bodily tastes which are plainly contrary to the spirit. Of the Spirit's threats to Natural Man.

When Natural Man saw the Spirit angered because he fed on these things and hoped still to feed on them, he was very ill content and spoke once more. He seemed to himself to have just cause for complaint, for he thought a little refreshment should not be denied him, especially spiritual refreshment such as this, for the Spirit had told him a time would come when he would be fed and satisfied by the things of the spirit. Now that he saw the Spirit would neither feed itself on spiritual things nor let him feed on them, he said:

NATURAL MAN: Thou hast broken thy promise, Spirit. It cannot be that I persevere when I am kept so strictly, without any bodily or spiritual comfort.

SPIRIT: I see that thou complainest, as it seems to thee with reason, and therefore I will satisfy thee. Thou hast not understood my words. It is true enough that I told thee thou wouldst at last be contented by all which contented me. But thou art looking not for contentment but for food. And I am not contented by these feelings; nay, I abhor them and would have thee abhor them too. Thou still hast thy instincts and tastes and thinkest I should provide for them. Know that I would destroy and rule them so that they gave thee no desires but such as pleased me. I bear in mind that thou art sick and would give thee only food for the sick, and what thou wouldst have is bad for thy health. Thou sayest that these are spiritual tastes, given by God, which can do no harm, but know that because thy senses have a part in thy understanding thy judgment is not good. My will is to be attentive only to pure and naked love, which can attach itself to nothing for which the creature has either bodily or spiritual taste or feelings. I would have thee know that I fear attachment to spiritual taste or feelings much more than to those which are bodily.

This is because the spiritual attaches man to it because it seems good, and without great difficulty he cannot be made to understand that it is other than good: thus he still feeds on what seems to come from God. But I tell thee that, in truth, he who desires only God must flee these things, for to pure love of God they are like poison. Spiritual tastes should be avoided more than the devil, for if they attack a man they give birth, unknown to him, to a sickness past curing. Believing he is in a good state, he is unaware that these tastes are a hindrance to perfect good, which is God Himself.

Bodily tastes, being plainly contrary to the spirit, cannot hide behind a good seeming, and therefore I fear them less. The contentment and peace I would give thee are those with which I will content myself and which I am sure will content thee too; but because thou art too soiled thou canst not have them yet.

First I will cleanse the house; then I will adorn it and fill it with good things which will content us both, but which will feed neither thee nor me. Thou sayest thou canst not bear this, but know that thou must, and what cannot be done in one year will be done in ten. Thy struggling troubles me not, for my will is to conquer in one way or another: I must rid my back of this goad of thine or I will never be at ease. Thou art gall to me and poison in all my meat, and until I have put thee down I will never fare well. Thou shewest thyself disposed to do thy worst: know that I, to be the sooner quit of thy works, will do as much; but my worst, which I will do to thee, will turn to thy benefit and profit. I warn thee not to fight me about this; far from fulfilling thy will and intent, thou wilt rather get their opposite. Comfort thyself then with patience, giving up all hope. Do my will now and at last I will do thine.

CHAPTER XVI

Natural Man begs the Spirit to do justice equitably, saying he has been no more than an instrument, the Spirit having been the first to sin. The Spirit proves the contrary to him. Of the cause of their fall. The Spirit shews Natural Man that they must cleanse themselves here below, for it is better to suffer for a thousand years here than one hour in Purgatory.

NATURAL MAN: I am, as thou seest, most dolorous and ill content, and neither by persuasion nor by force can I escape from doing thy will. But I pray thee to satisfy me on one point; thereafter thou shalt go on with that thou hast begun and I will be as patient as I can. O Spirit, thou who executest justice on me so severely, I pray thee at least to make thy justice just. Thou knowest that I am an animal body, without reason, power, will or memory, since all these things are in the Spirit; I work as an instrument, nor can I do other than what thou willest. Tell me, since thou wast the first to sin by reason and by will and I was thy instrument, bringing to effect sins already committed spiritually, which of us deserves punishment?

SPIRIT: Thy reasoning seems at first sight good, yet I will soon refute it to thy satisfaction, as thou wilt acknowledge. If, as thou sayest, thou Natural Man hadst never sinned and couldst not sin, then God, who wills that the body goes there where the soul goes, either to paradise or to hell, would deliver unjust judgment, for he who does neither good nor ill ought to receive neither punishment nor reward. Now since God cannot be unjust, it follows that this reasoning goes too far. I confess that I was the first to sin, for having free will I cannot be constrained against my will, and neither good nor evil can be done unless I first consent to it. When I turn to good, heaven and earth come to my help; from all sides I am moved to do good, and I can be hindered neither by demons nor by the world nor by the flesh.

When I turn to evil, help still comes to me from all sides, from the demons, from the world, and from myself, that is from the flesh and from the malignant instinct which man harbours in himself, being prone to evil. And since God rewards all that is good and punishes all that is evil, it must be concluded that all who work together for good will be rewarded and all who work together for evil punished. Thou knowest that at first I would have been attentive to my spiritual instinct and I began to follow it most vehemently, but thou didst so goad me to go counter to it, bringing forward so many reasons and making such a show of thy needs, that we had great disputes. Then came Self-love as a mediator, attaching himself to one or the other of us, and so defiling us both that, stooping to succour thee, I left the right path. Know that for this both of us will be justly punished. It is true that if that great wretchedness which is mortal sin were in us (which God forbid!) I would suffer more torment than thou, for I am the chief and the more noble. Then both of us would wish we had never been created.

It therefore behoves us to cleanse ourselves here below not only of all defilement but also of even the least imperfection brought on us by our bad habits. And I declare to thee that God has given me a light so piercing and clear that I am sure not the least stain will be left in me, in my soul or even in my body, unless this light fail me before we part.

Note well what I say to thee. How long thinkest thou this time for cleansing will last? Thou knowest well it may be short. At first the thing seems horrible to thee, but as thou goest forward thou wilt feel less pain because thy evil habits will be consumed; and if thou doubtest whether help to endure will be given thee, cease to fear and know that God, who has ordained in most holy wise, never suffers man to bear a burden for which he is not able. If we look for own good, we see that it will profit us more to be tried a little here below than ever afterwards to be in woe. It would be better to be tried for a thousand years by all the ills that can come to us in the flesh and in this world than to spend one hour in Purgatory. I have spoken these few words to thee to comfort thee.

CHAPTER XVII

*God pours and sheds a divine sweetness into the Soul, and
she cries out against this, wishing for no proofs of love.
Yet God ceases not to hold her sunk in the sea of divine
love. He gives her a sight of His most pure love and also
one of self-love and of her evil inclinations.*

When the Spirit had thus given Natural Man satisfaction, it left him and went back to its own first, clear
and pure object. Closely it followed its inmost and
piercing love, of which the bonds held it inwardly in
such an embrace that Natural Man had hardly leave
to breathe, whether the matter were spiritual or bodily,
and seemed beside himself.

God, having thus disposed this vessel for a pure
and clear love, began to tempt His creature with fit
and very spiritual temptations. He shed on her the great
sweetness and divine gentleness of a most gentle love,
and the Soul and the Body were so filled therewith
that it almost overwhelmed them. But the eye of love
sees everything, and no sooner did the Soul see these
things than she began to cry out and say she would have
none of this gentleness and savour in this life, and
cared not for this proof of love, for proof spoils love
itself.

I will protect myself as much as I can from this sweetness (said she) and will not draw near to it; I will grant
it no quiet and separate place in which I may feed
on it, for it is poison to pure love.

But God still kept her busied at the source of this
infinite gentleness. Albeit she still said she desired no
proofs of love, she was, none the less, ever sunk in the
sea of divine love, whereof she had not one but many
and divers visions.

In one of these visions God caused her to see a ray of the very pure love with which He loved her, and so mighty was this sight that if He had not tempered its loving fire by a vision of the self-love which had defiled her, she could not still have lived.

Another time He tempered this great fire by giving her a sight of herself, that is of her evil inclinations which were contrary to pure love. And seeing them, she would rather not have been than have offended God's love by the least sin or the smallest fault.

Now the Spirit, being thus busy, no longer gave a thought to its Natural Man, and had no more wish to think of him than if he had never been. Thus it rid itself of the burden of Natural Man and taught him what habits it would.

CHAPTER XVIII

Natural Man laments and asks to be allowed to do something. The Spirit consents and orders him to obey all men, and never to be stayed by his pleasure or displeasure from following the rule which the Spirit gives him. How the Spirit forbids him to make friends with any one person.

Natural Man, seeing his path straitened daily, again spoke to the Spirit and with the greatest fear and reverence said humbly:

NATURAL MAN: I see that thou hast taken from me all comfort in outward things, so that I may count myself dead to the world. If thou perseverest with this strictness, the time will come when I would rather die at once than live thus.

SPIRIT: I consent to give thee something to do outwardly so long as thou takest no pleasure in it. Thy works thou wilt abhor; if thou complainest, it will be the worse for thee.

NATURAL MAN: Anything will content me if but I do something.

SPIRIT: Know then that first I would have thee try what it is to be obedient; thou must become humble and submissive to every creature, and for practice in this thou shalt work for thy living. Moreover I would have thee visit the sick and the poor of all sorts whenever thou art called to do works of mercy, never refusing. Thou shalt do all for which I give thee an instinct, and thus thou shalt cleanse away the filth in which thou findest the sick, and when called to do this shalt leave all else, even though thou art speaking with God, and go forthwith to him who calls thee and whither thou art led. Never shalt thou consider who it is who calls thee or what thou goest to do. I would have thee never make a choice; rather must another's will be thine; never must thou follow thine own will.

I will keep thee at these exercises while I judge it needful, for I would destroy in thee all the disorder which comes of the pleasure or displeasure thou mayest have in this life. I would rid thee of all imperfection, and would have joy or pain stay thee no more than if thou wert dead. Of this I shall make sure by proving thee, for I shall put thee to the trials which seem to me needed. If I perceive, when I put thee to work which is abhorrent, that thou feelest or seest it, then I shall keep thee at it until thou feelest or seest it no longer. And I say no less of whatsoever may be of comfort to thee; I shall make thee embrace its opposite until thou neither seest nor feelest anything to be agreeable or pleasing. The better to make these trials, I shall put thee both to what may please and to what may displease thee. Nor would I have thee make friends with anyone or have special affection for any of thy kin; I would have thee love all men, poor and rich, friends and kinsmen, without love or affection, not distinguishing one man from another or making friends with anyone, however religious and spiritual. Nor shalt

thou go into any house out of friendship; it is enough
that thou goest (as I have said) when thou art called.
This is the rule I would have thee keep in thy conversation with creatures on the earth.

CHAPTER XIX

*Of the poverty in which the Spirit made Natural Man
live. How the Spirit made him visit the poor and the sick.
How he found himself in the midst of calamities. Of the
oppression and the inward attacks he felt.*

The Spirit, having spoken thus to Natural Man,
put the thing into practice in this way. First, it made
the creature of whom I speak so poor that she could not
have lived if God had not provided for her by alms.
Then, whenever the Ladies of Mercy, after their wont,
asked her to render divers services to the poor, she
went with them, and came upon creatures filled with
every sort of filth and covered with vermin, whose
stink was hardly to be borne. Such was the calamitous
and wretched state of some of the sick that they uttered
fearful words of despair. When she went into these
places it seemed to her that she entered the grave;
any natural man would have been afraid. Yet this
creature touched these sick, to give some refreshment
to their souls and bodies. Sometimes she came upon
sick people who not only stank and were filthy but also
bemoaned themselves unceasingly, complaining with vile
insults of those who served them. She went, too, to visit
the poor of Saint Lazarus's Hospital, and there found
very great suffering; it was as though the Spirit sent her
to seek out everything calamitous and wretched. So
it was that she found herself far worse off while she did
these exercises than she had foreseen. Then she felt she
had to fight a twofold fight, with Natural Man who

abhorred the misery he saw, and with the inward busyness in which the Spirit, being remote from outward impressions, kept her; she had no time for conversation with anyone.

Her Natural Man, thus terrified by the Spirit, was continually importuned and knew not what course to take. When he felt the Spirit besieging him, anything seemed better to him than to withstand it; when he saw misery, he felt that he wished to flee it but could not. All this seemed to him too much, especially when he saw that the creature's Spirit was having its will, so that she went through these exercises without disgust, and would put abominations into her mouth, if need were, as though she were eating bread.[1] This poor Natural Man found himself thus reduced to the last extremity and saw no help for it. Whoever had seen him in this utmost conflict would have had great compassion on him. But all seemed easy to the Spirit, since all was being done that it might be free, and it put these things into practice with full effect.

CHAPTER XX

Natural Man, having tried the two paths of outward misery and of inward oppression, is allowed by the Spirit to choose between them. How when he grew sick at the sight of a rotten thing, the Spirit made him eat some of it.

When the Spirit had caused Natural Man to make trial of all the aforesaid misery, and had let him understand all it wanted of him, it said to him:

---

[1] It is impossible not to be shocked by this practice of the saint's. But we must bear in mind both that she lived in the latter half of the fifteenth century which was ignorant of sanitation and well used to dirt, and that her reaction against the luxury, greed and epicureanism of her class in Renascence Genoa was extreme, leading her to eschew fastidiousness about anything material. In her disregard for physical cleanliness she contrasts with two great saints only a few years posterior to her in date who valued it highly, Saint Theresa of Avila and Saint Ignatius Loyola. In part, perhaps, because they were citizens of that austere country Spain, cleanliness was to them not a luxury but an avoidance of sloth.

SPIRIT: Now that thou knowest in practice what words did not make thee see clearly, what meanest thou to do? Thou hast tried the two paths open to thee. I consent to thy choosing which of them it pleases thee to follow. But learn that I will make thee live among creatures in great subjection for as long as I like, for my will is that thou have no place in this world in which to turn round and take the least rest. And I will put what I say into practice forthwith.

NATURAL MAN: I have seen and tried the two paths which both lead me to extremity. Great and abominable though the misery be which I have seen, understood and tried, I think I would rather live therewith than be besieged by the divine ray. But I fear to suffer in both ways, that is to endure misery outwardly and the divine assault inwardly, and therefore I am in great anguish.

SPIRIT: Know that when thou hast one of these things thou wilt not have the other. But I warn thee that it is my will to take from thee all that is superfluous, so that I may live, as much as I can, in the purity and radiance in which I was created, and I shall make nothing of any hindrance to this end.

NATURAL MAN: Seeing thee so decided, it seems to me that to say more would be waste of time. I give in wholly to thy will; I put myself in thy hands as though I were dead, alive though I be; but I hope to die.

And from this time, whenever Natural Man came upon filth or vermin, and handling it wanted to vomit, the Spirit, to reduce him more and more, said to him: "Take some of this vermin, put it in thy mouth and eat it if thou wouldst be rid of thy sickness." When Natural Man heard these words he was a little shocked but soon resolved to do the thing, and as he obeyed he was indeed rid of his disgust, for by forcing himself to obey the order without question he came from that time to swallow the vermin or other refuse as though it were a medicine, and indeed it healed him of his anguish and sickness. So afterwards he made nothing of it, and freely put filth in his mouth as though he handled precious pearls.

Thereafter the Spirit shewed him yet other misery, that of people who had incurable ulcers and who stank so that to stay near them was a thing hardly to be borne. But the Spirit gave him the instinct to do all that was needful, and with this corrupted flesh he had to do as he had done with the vermin of which we have spoken.[1]

These things were so contrary to Natural Man that by nature he could not have accomplished them. But when he had done violence to himself he was left in a contentment which made his courage for the future greater and greater, and enabled him to bear with impatient and desperate people, and otherwise to deny himself. These things the Spirit made him do for about three years, and at the same time the creature was ever kept inwardly busy, so that she did these outward things without any feeling which corresponded to them. The Spirit made her persevere until it was sure she cared nothing for these things which she did.

CHAPTER XXI

The Spirit caused the creature's Natural Man to dwell in a hospital, where she served as a maid, obeying every order given her. And when she had become used to things she naturally abhorred, she was made governess of the hospital and received the prudence needed for the discharge of this office. The loving faith which grew in her without ceasing.

The Spirit ordered the creature to practise another exercise which greatly subjected her mind and body, as follows. She was required to dwell with her husband

[1] See the note on page 80.

in a hospital so as to serve in it. This she did, and there she was subjected to those who governed the hospital as though she had been their servant. She hardly dared speak; she stayed quiet with her husband in one of the rooms and submitted to everything put on her. What she was charged to do she did with all diligence, although the dwellers in the hospital treated her as though she were of no account. Never did anything awaken in her any feeling corresponding to itself, for she was rapt from all earthly things. Then Natural Man said to the Spirit:

NATURAL MAN: If it be thy will that I practise these exercises, make me able for them. I refuse nothing, but it is needful that I have, as by accident, a little liking for the work I do or it will be ill directed.

And a feeling, with and by which the creature worked, was given to Natural Man. But it was granted only so far as it was needed, at the moment at which she worked and for the work she did; afterwards the feeling and the memory of the work done were taken from her. For many years the Spirit kept her at such exercises in great poverty.

When the Spirit had tried this Natural Man by the aforesaid misery and subjection, and saw itself entirely his master, having proved him with trials he had at first abhorred but which now sickened him no longer, so that he busied himself without weariness or repulsion on mean and repulsive tasks (like the aforesaid), then the Spirit put him to another trial by making the creature superior of the hospital, to govern and rule it. To see whether any esteem she gained aroused the element of self in her, the Spirit held her at this exercise for many years, during which she was suffered to keep her wits about her and have the memory she needed, and was helped by the Spirit without whom she would have fallen short. And throughout this work she still kept her interior life uninvaded, for her love had secretly grown as her Natural Man had been reduced to nothing.

For as more and more she lost the habit of self-love, she came more and more to have pure and clear love, and the more this entered into her and abode with her, the more it caused her to destroy Natural Man. Thus this Soul, on fire with love, was burnt up in the loving fire of God, which grew without ceasing so that more and more was she consumed. She rendered services very swiftly and never rested, for thus she distracted herself from this fire which each day besieged her more. She could speak of it to no one but discoursed of it only to herself and unheard.

Then the Spirit, who had thus held this creature, said: "Henceforth I will not call her a human creature, for I see that she is all in God and without Natural Man."

END OF PART I OF THE DIALOGUE

PART II

CHAPTER I

Of a new love which God poured and shed on the creature's heart, whereby He drew to Himself the Spirit who was followed by the Soul. How the powers of the Soul were almost drowned and sunk in this love. How the Body, being subject to the Soul, was left as though lost and outside his natural being.

After this creature had been stripped of the world, the flesh, her goods, her exercises, her affections and all things else except God alone, God willed to take from her herself also, separating the Soul from the Spirit terribly and with sharpest suffering, in a way hardly to be told or understood by any who have not themselves experienced it in the light of God. He poured into this creature's heart a new love, so subtle and so vehement that it drew the Soul with all her powers to Him, in suchwise that she was taken out of her natural being. So unceasingly busy was she kept by this new love that she could take delight in nothing and look neither heavenward nor earthward.

This Soul could no longer respond to the feelings of the Body, who therefore was all but beside himself, confused, astonied, and not knowing where he was nor what he should do or say. In this new way, not yet understood or known by any creature, new and unknown works were then done. It was, as I shall tell, as though a chain joined the creature's Spirit to God. For God,

who is Spirit, drew her Spirit to Him, and it stayed
in God and in Him was busied. The Soul followed the
Spirit because she could not be without it; and because
she could not live without it, was kept busy in God,
and stayed in Him while He kept the Spirit in Himself.
The Body, which was subject to the Soul, was left as
though lost and beside himself, for he could not find
natural food by his senses, being fed only by means
of the Soul which was no longer responsive to him.
Only the Spirit was still almost itself, tending to the end
for which God created it; stripped and naked it abode
in God and was kept in Him so long as He pleased,
saving that the Body was suffered still to live. Afterwards the Soul and the Body went back to the works
natural to them, but when they had been restored
by the Spirit's rest, God again drew the Spirit to work
as before, and thus all animal imperfections were consumed little by little.

In this way the Soul of which I speak was purged
of her evil habits and inclinations, and was left pure
and fit to unite with her Spirit, at its own time and
unhindered. God did this work only out of His love,
which was so great that it worked unceasingly to profit
and serve this His well beloved Soul.

The Soul had no part in this work of God of which
I speak. He filled her with a secret love which took
from her all her natural being. Thus the work was
supernatural, being wrought in the sea of this secret
love, which is so great that everyone borne into it stays
in it as though he were drowned and dead. This love
passes understanding, memory and will, which powers
of this Soul were plunged into the sea of divine love,
and were so drawn out of their own state which they
had when the Soul was created, that if anything but this
love had been presented to them it would have been
hell to them.

Thus this Soul had, while still in this life, her part in
some degree with the blessed, but unknown to herself,

for so great and high a thing could not be understood, being beyond her powers. Yet her powers were busy only about this love, and plunged in this subtle love were contented. And when any spoke to her of created things, these seemed to her stupid, without strength or virtue; she knew not where they were to be found. All this work stayed hidden in God, and ever it grew so that the Spirit was made yet happier and more able to bear all that God disposed for it. Nor was it attentive to anything else, for the Soul, as though dead, neither meddled with the work nor knew of it.

But since God willed to draw the Soul by means of the Body to the perfection for which He had ordained her, how could the Body still live on earth, as he had to do, when he had been made strange to his natural way of being? The Body could not use his understanding, memory or will for worldly things, nor could he delight in spiritual things, and therefore he lived in great torment. But God, who had taken charge of the Body, would have none but Himself meddle in the matter, and did as I shall tell.

CHAPTER II

Of the way God took when His love had made seizure. Of the Body's weakness and of the help given him by created things. Of the greatness of the pain suffered by Natural Man, of which he complains without complaint, being inwardly agreeable to God's will. How sweet, how severe and yet how merciful, is Purgatory in this life.

Sometimes God lightened this hold His love had taken, letting the Spirit breathe and respond to the Soul and the Soul to the Body, and then the feelings of the Soul and the Body were fit to receive some comfort from created things and thus were given life. But

when God withdrew the Spirit to Himself all the rest
followed, for then the Body was left as though dead,
and was so strange to his natural way of being that
when he came back to it he was utterly weak nor could
be helped by created things. Natural Man could neither
eat nor drink nor make a sign of life; almost he was past
feeling; he had to be governed like a little child who
can but weep; and, what was even worse, he could
take no pleasure in what nature desires, for all taste
had been taken from him, having been violently drawn
out of his nature. When the Soul had been thus for some
time, she turned to her Lord with a great lament, saying
to Him:

SOUL: O my Lord, hitherto I was in great peace,
contentment and delight, for all my powers enjoyed
the love Thou gavest me, and it seemed to them that
they were in paradise. But now they are as though
driven out of their dwelling, in a country unknown
to them where all is contrary to their wonted way of
life. At first my understanding, my memory and my
will felt Thy love in every work done as Thou didst
ordain, and were greatly satisfied as were all with whom
I went; Thy sweet conversation with me gave a savour
to all things. But now I am naked and stripped of all
things, and without power to love or work after my wont.
What then can I do who am at once alive and dead,
without understanding, memory or will and, what is
worse, without love! Except with love I thought I could
not live, for man is created for love and delight, and above
all for love of God and delight in Him, who is our first
object and our end.

This new work, which I see being done, takes love
and delight from me, and I am lost in myself, not knowing
what to do or say. O how hard and unbearable this
way of life seems to me, the more because my powers
are agreed among themselves, having found rest in their
object and end, which is God! Albeit they are ignorant
of this work, yet in their ignorance they are satisfied.

But how can Natural Man live, forsaken and alone? He is left dry, naked and without strength; he has eyes and cannot see, a nose and cannot smell, ears and cannot hear, a mouth and cannot taste, a heart and cannot love. All his ways of living are imprisoned in this secret love, but he cannot live by it; nay, rather he gets death by it. He is in his own home, with all his feelings quick and whole, and cannot use them as others do.

Natural Man too bemoaned himself and said:

NATURAL MAN: What shall I do, wretch that I am, left alone in the world? I shall live in despair and none shall have pity on me, for the work which is being wrought will not be known to be of God; almost always I must go contrary to the ways of other men, whether religious or in the world; the things I have to do will be deemed madness. No order, no method is left to my living; I will seem to shew a bad example rather than edify men.

Alas, alas, how cruel to Natural Man is this work I see! It is as though I were in a burning furnace with my mouth sealed. I can neither live nor die; it seems that I must be turned to ashes; nor may I complain, for inwardly I am agreeable to the will of God which works thus as He has ordained, beyond my understanding and even that of the Soul. What He does is shewn as He executes the work. It is Natural Man who feels the torment, yet he may not complain; if he could but complain he would be refreshed.

O how sweet and how cruel is that purgatory on earth, where it is not known for what it is! How sweet compared to the Purgatory of the other life! Cruel it seems to us who are blind, who see the body martyred almost past bearing. By him who has the light it is seen to be wrought out of love; he who is blind flees it. Since we, being all sinners, cannot flee it for ever, how much better it is for us to be purged here than in the other life! For he who is purged in this world, by his own free will and the grace shed on him, pays less than a

penny in a thousand pounds. Never does God subject
man to this working without his consent; for one instant
God leaves the choice to men, who accepts the work
by his free will and puts himself in God's hands that
God may do as He pleases. But his natural man is
given no inkling of what is toward.

This consent having been given in the spirit, God
binds the soul to Himself by a bond never broken.
All this is done without natural man, who must still
be subject to God's ordinance and to the spirit's choice.
Finding himself thus in subjection, natural man howls
as animals do when they are hurt; and since he knows
not what is the end of all this, he is suffered to cry, while
God, not heeding his groans and laments, still does
God's work.

CHAPTER III

*Natural Man, being under threat, wishes to know why,
and is promised that he will know. How God, in search
of men, draws them by divine means and inspirations.
Of the unceasing sorrow of the creature and how, thus
afflicted, she cries to God, who gives her life with a ray
of His love. She sees the grace God has done her and
is again wounded by love. Of her confession and her
contrition.*

Natural man, seeing himself under threat of divers
martyrdoms which he must suffer, and being unable
to defend himself, wished to know why he deserved
so great a torment in which he could hope for no help.
The answer sent to his mind was that this grace of
knowledge would be granted him at the right time.
Thus men condemned to death have the sentence
passed on their crimes read to them, and thereafter bear
their shameful death more patiently, whereby many
of them are saved.

"Of My infinite love", said God, "I go unceasingly in search of souls to lead them to eternal life; with My light I enlighten them, moving their free will in many and divers ways; and when man accepts Me and consents to be inspired by Me, then I let more of My light shine in him, and he sees that he is like one shut up in a dark stable, deep in mire, surrounded by many venomous animals who seek his death. All of which he had not before perceived, having been in darkness. He knows too that of himself he cannot get out, and seeing, thanks to My light, that he is in so great danger, he cries to Me, asking that of My mercy I will deliver him from the wretchedness which on all sides enfolds him. Then more and more do I enlighten him, and he, having more light, knows yet better in what peril he is. Yet more loudly does he cry on Me, shedding very bitter tears and saying: 'O my God, take me out of this place and then do with me all Thou wilt! I will bear all things if but Thou wilt deliver me who am in the midst of such great misery and danger.'"

It seemed to the creature of whom I speak that God was deaf to her cries. Yet day by day He gave her more light; and more and more, each day, was she consumed, for as the light shone more bright[1] she saw her danger more clearly, nor had she any hope of escape. For a long time God let her cry out and answered not her cries. But she still persevered, His love being infused in her, and a hidden fire having been kindled in her by the sight of her faults. For a time she was kept as in chains by her unhappiness and engrossed by it. Unceasing and deep pain was her only food, the more because the grace and light vouchsafed her were ever growing. Thus her flesh and blood and all the superfluous humours which were in her were burnt away, and she became so weak and afflicted that she could no longer move. Utterly left to herself, she cried to God: *Miserere mei Deus secundum magnam misericordiam tuam.*

---

[1] That is, the danger described in the preceding paragraph.

And God, when He saw that she gave herself up wholly
to His mercy and despaired of herself, put life into her
by a ray of His love, and at the same time let a new
light shine for her by which she saw the gravity of her
faults, such that hell should have been their payment,
and saw too the singular grace which God had vouchsafed her. She was left in this life with the wound of a
new love and of sorrow for her offences against God's
great goodness, and she began to confess her sins with
admirable contrition. She would have done any penance
she could for them, with her soul and her body.

To be contrite, to confess, to make satisfaction: these
are the first works of the soul after God has given it
light; by these it is stripped of all vices and sins and
clothed in virtue; and in this state it is kept until it has
learnt the habit of virtue.

CHAPTER IV

*God pours and sheds in the creature's heart another ray of
love which fills her soul. Her body is restored, and all is love
and exceeding great joy while all love lower than God
is consumed.*

Then God shed on the creature another ray of love
which filled her soul, and was so abundant that her
body too was restored, and she felt only love and heart's
joy so that she thought herself in Paradise. She was kept
in this state until all love lower than God had been
consumed in her and she was left with love for God
alone and in Him was all recollected. God vouchsafed
many graces to this creature, sending her very pleasant
savours on which she and all her friends in God were
fed, and words of love like burning arrows which pierced
the hearts of those who heard her. Even her body was,
through her mind, set on fire; it seemed as though her

soul would leave her body to join what she loved. The time was one of great peace and contentment in which the creature fed only on life eternal.

In this state there is no fear of suffering or hell, of anything untoward or of adversity; with this love everything seems easy to bear. O loving and joyous heart! O happy soul that has enjoyed this love! No longer canst thou taste or see aught else, for this is thy country for which thou wast created. O most sweet unknown love, whoever has tasted thee can never again be without thee! O man, thou who art created for this love, how couldst thou ever be content without it? How be at rest or live? In this love thou findest all thou desirest, and such is thy satisfaction that it can be neither told nor thought. Only he who has felt it can understand anything of it. O love, in thee all joys and savours are met together; in thee all desires are satisfied!

He who would tell what the heart feels which is in love with God would break all other hearts, were they harder than the diamond and more obstinate than the devil. O flame of love, thou burnest away all rust, thou drivest from the soul all the darkness of faults; so subtly thou workest that the least shadow of imperfection cannot endure before thee! So dost thou work that the soul is cleansed of what cannot be seen except by thy eyes which see faults where others see perfection. O love, who cleansest and consumest our imperfections, who givest light and strength to our feelings! Thou knowest what we must do, Thou who, without being loved by us, art pure love.

Then this Soul, stupefied by the sight of God thus loving her so deeply, said:

CHAPTER V

The Soul asks what love is. Our Lord answers her in part, speaking to her of the greatness, the qualities, the properties and the causes and effects of His love.

SOUL: O Lord, what is this Soul of which Thou hast such care, on which Thou settest so great a price and which we hold so cheaply? O were it but given me to know the cause of Thy so great and pure love for a creature who has reason and yet so often goes against Thee!

The Lord, partly answering her prayer, answered thus:

THE LORD: If thou knewest how much I love thee, thou couldst never know anything more in this life, for it will kill thee; or if indeed thou still didst live, it would be by a miracle. And if thou sawest thy wretchedness clearly, knowing My goodness and the great and pure love with which I never cease to work for man, thou wouldst live in despair. For such is my love that it would destroy not only the body but the soul too, if that were possible. My love is infinite and I cannot but love what I have created; My love is pure, simple and clear; with this love only can I love.

To whomsoever understood the least spark of My love all other love would seem false, as in truth it is. The cause of My love is no other than that love itself. And since thou art not able to understand it, abide in peace nor seek what thou canst not find. This love of Mine is best known by an inward feeling. A man gets it when, by its working, it separates him from what in him is man, for man is his own hindrance. This love burns up his malignity and rids him of it, rendering him fit to know and understand what love is.

O admirable and stupendous is the work of the love God gives man so that he may do what he must in order to reach the perfection for which he is ordained! God also grants him the graces and light he needs, in suchwise and such quantity that he never has more nor less than he needs. For if he had not enough, he might excuse himself for not having worked, saying he lacked grace; and if he had too much, he would be justly punished for not using all he had.

Grace is multiplied as a man uses it; when works increase, so does grace, and when works do not increase, then neither does grace. Thus it is clear that from one moment to another God gives man what he needs, neither more nor less, to each one according to his degree and capacity. And God does all this of His love and for man's profit. But we are cold and in our works neglectful; and since the spirit has the instinct to reach perfection swiftly, it seems to us that grace has failed us, albeit it never fails. If we do not work now according to the measure of the grace we have, more grace is not given us for the future, and the fault is ours alone.

O wretched man, how canst thou excuse thyself for not repaying worthily the great care with which God has ever provided for thee and so lovingly provides for thee still? Thou wilt see and understand His care better when thou comest to die. Then wilt thou be struck dumb and astonied; knowing then the truth, thou wilt have nought to say in thy own defence. Thou wilt be put to great confusion because thou hast been unwilling to do good works, so much helped as thou hast been, so much grace and love as thou hast had from thy Lord, who to answer thy other questions says to thee:

CHAPTER VI

God declares that he makes the body a purgatory for the soul in this world. Of man's need to renounce himself and sink himself wholly in God, and of the wretchedness of the man who is busied over other things when he has only this life in which to merit.

THE LORD: It is by experience rather than by thy reason that thou canst understand the cause of the great sufferings thou must undergo. Yet know this at least: I make thy body a purgatory for thy soul; in this way I increase the soul's glory, drawing it to Myself without other purgatory, and to do this I knock unceasingly at the door of man's heart. If he consent to open to Me, I lead him, with unceasing and loving care, to that degree of glory for which I created him. If he could know my care for his benefit and profit, he would give himself to Me, leaving all else though all My creation were his.

Rather than lose My loving care, which leads him to supreme glory, he would willingly endure martyrdom of any kind whatsoever. But My will is that man give himself to Me only for love's sake and with faith, to which love and faith fear and the things which belong to himself are contrary. For these dwell in self-love which cannot stand beside My pure and simple love, in which man's spirit must be sunk so that he may never be taken out of My care. Without My care he may not enter the pure, clear and simple abyss of My being, for it would be a great hell to him. And since man cannot cleanse his soul otherwise or at another time than in this life, is he not most wretched and mad to busy himself over other things, and to lose this precious time given him only for this end, when he can never have another time and when, once it is past, it can never return? Heaken then, O Soul most dear, hearken to My voice; open thine ears to thy Lord who loves thee so and does so much good to thee, wrapt as thou art in multitudinous sin, sunk in such wretchedness, burdened with so many evil habits. My light will make thee see thy sins and know their gravity, of thine own experience, when thou art delivered from them.

THE SOUL: Lord, Thou hast given me many reasons for all I have endured and still have to endure. But give me, I pray Thee, if it please Thee, a reason for this suffering which satisfies my understanding. I have great need thereof for I feel the vehemence of Thy love coming upon me.

THE LORD: Thou knowest that when, of thine own free will, thou didst yield to Me, thou wast so defiled that without My providence thou wouldst have been condemned to hell, for thou hadst been led, as one dead, into the wretchedness of sin. I provided thee with light and contrition, by the help of which thou didst make thy confession. Since then thou hast done many penances, said prayers and given alms for a long time, in satisfaction for thy sins. I suffered thee to struggle and grieve until thou wast strong enough not to fall again. Then I made thee practise a thousand virtues of which thou hast so taken the habit that now thou delightest in them and hast indeed no other delights.

At this time this Soul began to delight in spiritual things; and many temptations which came to her made her practised in the Lord's ways. And she saw how God often provided for her in the midst of many and divers oppressions and tribulations put on her by men, the world and the demons, and by herself who had evil habits. Against all these enemies she had to fight until all her bad habits, whether inward or outward, had been consumed, for it is bad habits which make war on men. If it were not for them, none would ever be tempted except that he might receive more grace, and temptation would be almost without peril, for God, who for love of us suffered us to be tempted, would sustain us under temptation.

CHAPTER VII

The Soul, clothed anew in virtue, began to take breath in Our Lord. God shewed her the work of love He had wrought in her, of His goodness only and to set her free. Whereat, as the Soul acknowledged her wretchedness, a fire which did not abate was kindled in her, and she could neither speak nor think of aught else.

When God had rid this Soul of her bad habits and clothed her in virtue, and when, being learned in the spiritual way, she had begun a little to take breath in her Lord (as one withdrawn from the battle and freed from servitude), then she was in great contentment. For God opened her eyes and shewed her how much He had helped her and had defended her against her many visible and invisible enemies, and against herself who was the worst of them all. Then the Soul, seeing all God's care and the loving work of His hand, and feeling herself inwardly all relieved of her past affliction, began to turn to her Lord; and He, wishing to draw her to a higher state, made her see, with the eye of divine love, more loving work which His great and solicitous care had accomplished in her. Then she was astounded and amazed as she saw and considered what God was and what she was, a wretched, unhappy soul, sunk in such misery that only God's goodness had delivered her by His pure and simple love, and had, by pure and loving ways and means, made her fit to receive this divine love. This sight made her cry out, confessing her wretchedness and sins; and the love which God had shewn her kept her ever on fire, so that she could neither speak nor think of aught else. Thus she stayed until all other loves spiritual or bodily, had been burnt away.

For the more one is restricted to the love of God, so that it is unhindered by other loves, the greater it is and the more busied with it is the soul, for ever it grows and ever it secretly works on others and within the soul. This Soul, being in this state, enjoyed all things in peace and love and delight, outward and inward. And because she was near the path along which God would lead her, but knew it not yet, God said to her:

CHAPTER VIII

Our Lord shews the Soul how she had merited nothing at all, for she had spent on her purgation the time given her to grow in grace and glory, and how without His help she could not have done anything.

THE LORD: My daughter, hitherto thou hast followed My sweetness and My scents which have guided and borne thee in all the paths thou hast travelled, but without My help thou couldst have done nothing. On those paths thou hast, by My grace, purged thee of thy sins and rid thee of thy affections; thou hast clothed thee in virtue and the fire of love has been lit in thee, in which love thou art, as it were, joined to Me; such delight hast thou had, inwardly and outwardly, that almost thou thinkest thyself to be in Paradise.

But I declare to thee that hitherto thou hast no merit, for what thou hast done thou wast bound to do.[1] By

[1] It is Catholic doctrine that those who are in the state of grace, do merit by actions which they are bound to do and by actions done before they have paid their debt of temporal punishment, but this merit is due not to the nature of those actions considered in themselves but to God's positive decree and gracious dispensation. Apart from sanctifying grace, which is itself a purely gratuitous gift of God to man, and apart from God's free promise to accept acts done in grace as meritorious, they would not be such, since they are of themselves strictly due from the creature to the

My light thou sawest that thy penances, fasts, almsgiving and prayers were needed to pay all thy debts, and since thou hadst not wherewith to make satisfaction for them, what thou didst lack was given thee out of love, that thou mightest pay in full. Know that all this time thou hast spent in making satisfaction for thy sins is, as it were, lost, for it was time given thee to grow in grace and glory. Hitherto therefore thou hast no merit although it seems to thee that thou hast done great things; such are they deemed by those who know them not.

Moreover thou couldst not but clothe thee in virtues, for virtues draw love, and thus defend thee against vices and make thee fit to receive more light. And knowing thee not fit for this of thyself, nor skilled for any good work, I gave thee, that thou mightest work and persevere in working, a hidden love, by means of which thy powers and the feelings of thy body were so disposed that they willingly made satisfaction. I taught thee to love Me, for I willed to rid thee of every other love, and thereafter I led thee to the door of My true and perfect love. No further hast thou gone, for to go on would pass thy understanding and be beyond thy powers. Thou, who hast the instinct to go further, art not content with all thou hast done, but thou knowest not what thou shouldst choose to do.

CHAPTER IX

The Spirit, seeing the Soul led to the door of divine love, resolves to make both her and the Body suffer much, and tells her that it would be parted from her, and that to return to her former purity she must endure great martyrdom.

When the Spirit saw that the Soul, thus led to the door of divine love, could neither turn back nor go forward,

Creator, according to Christ's words: When you have done all these things that are commanded you, say, we are unprofitable servants: we have done that which we ought to do. Luke xvii. 10.

having been led as far as she could go by God with much
help from Him, and that she was kept by Him happy
in every part of her, yet not satisfied, then the Spirit said:

SPIRIT: Now the time has come for me to do to the Soul
what once she did to me. For many years I was subject
to her, and the door of my house was shut on me more
cruelly than can be told. For the Soul was so entangled
and kept down by the things of this world that, try as I
would, I could not rise to the height of my spiritual
works. I sought help from the goad of death, the fear
of hell and the hope of Paradise, from sermons, the
suffrages of the Church and divine inspirations, and
from sickness, poverty and other worldly tribulations,
hoping that, forsaken by all worldly things and lacking
every other help, she might in her extreme need have
recourse to God. Sometimes, in the extremity of her
need, she indeed turned to Him and promised to do
great things if He would help her. But when the moment
had passed, she returned to her wonted ways and I
was forced back to my prison. This came to pass very
often.

Now that I see the creature led, with all the feelings
of the Soul and the Body, so far that she can neither go
forward nor turn back, I will subject and imprison
Soul and Body lest they again prevent and hinder me.
Let them howl as they will; they will be at my mercy as
I was at the Soul's. Very ill she treated me, for never
did I receive the least comfort from my own country
that was not, at that instant, smothered by all the enemies
I had about me. Now I will keep the creature confined
and in subjection and cause her to undergo all the
suffering she can bear; never shall I have the least pity
on her. I have her in my hands and will make her so
naked, dry and forlorn that she will not have whither
to turn, saving indeed to supply the needs of life so that
she may not die but may still suffer a martyrdom which
shall be unknown to all and past curing. My will is
that not one of her members escape martyrdom until

my will be well accomplished. Whoever sees her thus in woe will wish for her death, as a less evil, and so would she do herself if she could without sin.

SOUL: I have heard thy great threats and been made aware of what I have to suffer. But I have not yet learnt the reason why I must bear all this, and I was promised that this would be told me.

SPIRIT: I would be parted from thee, and will answer thee now in words, but later I will do it far better in deeds by causing thee to go through what will make thee envy the dead. Thou hast been led to the door of God's love in many gentle ways and by divine graces with which thou hast clothed thyself. Thou hast stolen them and made them thine own, and so subtly are they hidden in thee that thou art not aware of them. So long have such thefts been thy wont that they are unseen of all eyes lower than God's, and thou thyself wouldst not believe any who told thee of them. But little by little thou wilt, by experience, learn and know that thou hast taken for thine own some of the first light given thee, and hast done no less with contrition, confession and satisfaction, prayers and other virtuous works, the outward and the inward stripping of thyself, the sweet love of God, and detachment from all things giving rise to bodily feelings, which feelings seem to be wholly dead in thee because they have been overcome by the divine.working. And since thy powers were long fed on all these works (for which thy feelings were the means), thou wast left filled with the love of God, and strong, so that often thou didst think thyself in Paradise. Inwardly thou hadst joy of all these things as though they were thine own, given thee by God for merit, nor didst thou render them to God, wholly and keeping nothing back, most simply and clearly, as thou shouldst have done. Thus wast thou a thief, and therefore art thou still defiled, and must suffer all the ills foretold and shewn thee. Know that there is much to do when God would cleanse a soul here below and bring it back to its first purity without suffering it to pass through another purgatory beyond this life, above all when His will is to draw it to some high degree of glory. For then the soul must not only be cleansed but must also win merit by great and manifold suffering.

And when the time had come, it pleased God to imprison this Spirit, keeping it shut up so closely in itself that it could no longer answer the Soul nor the Soul answer the Body. The creature was left wholly naked and dry, so that it was a wonder to live thus, especially at first, for although God drew the Soul secretly and little by little, it was to pass from one extreme to the other.[1] But at last the fire was lit and then, as when a cannon has been fired and the flame and powder are lost for ever, so this creature was left. She was like a fiddle without strings: once with the feelings of her soul and body she had made sweetest music and delighted all men; now she was held down, stripped and naked. Then when the Soul saw herself so narrowly besieged by the Spirit and was, because of the threats made to her, without hope of deliverance, she cried out to God and said:

CHAPTER X

The Soul acknowledged her need to make satisfaction willingly. It seemed to her that she had been forsaken by God and she asked for some person to help her. How Natural Man was put to the trial with which he was threatened. Of the martyrdom suffered by the Body when Body and Spirit were no longer responsive, the one to the other.

SOUL: Lord, I see that I must cleanse me of my thefts of Thy spiritual graces, and I begin to know that having willingly, by the Body, delighted in sin, I must make

[1] One extreme is natural humanity, the other is God and a share in God's life.

satisfaction therefore willingly and with sorrow, in my
feelings and in those of the Body, so as to pay what I
owe to the last farthing. I see that I have secretly stolen
from Thee what is Thine, and have very complacently
made many spiritual graces mine own and delighted
in them, nor counted them always Thine as I should
have done. Thus it has been with many sweetnesses
felt by me, of speech, hearing, taste and many others.
I see clearly how grave are these thefts, of the gravest
there can be because what I stole is very diverse from
man's wretchedness, for which nothing good is fit except
it please Thee to give it to him of Thy grace. It behoves
us to acknowledge that all grace comes from Thee, or
else we are thieves. And this theft has its beginning
in the devil, who tempts us without ceasing and by whom
many are deceived.

But how can I make satisfaction for this great and
subtle sin when neither strength nor feeling of soul or
body is left me? It is a hard thing to live in this world,
and yet live I must, enduring great martyrdom, that
I may purge me of my faults. It seems to me that divine
help has forsaken me; or if indeed I feel it, my feeling
is known only to Thee, my God. Yet still I would get
me to my thieving. Forsaken on all sides as I am, grant
me at least, O my Lord, one to understand and comfort
me in the torment which I see coming on me, even as
condemned men are given helpers lest they despair.

Then God somewhat comforted Natural Man, yet
soon put him to the trial with which he had been
threatened, and so, little by little, that Body fell sick.
And since the Body and the Spirit were no longer
responsive the one to the other (the Spirit keeping
the powers of the Soul in suspense and busy), the Body
was left stripped, arid and dry and knew not that the
work was God's. Thus he was burnt away. Each thing
he suffered gave him lively pain, and his sickness still
worsened, and if God had not kept the creature inwardly
busy, she could not have borne this sickness. But to help

her outwardly, according to her needs, God gave her a religious who understood the divine working and comforted her much. For of his own nature, Natural Man could not have lived in the midst of the manifold and harsh martyrdom he suffered, which was such as cannot be told by human tongue, or if it were told it would not be understood even by one who with his own eyes had seen the suffering, the inward martyrdom being infinitely greater than that which was outward; and no cure for it being known. On some days God comforted Natural Man, leaving him without pain, so that the creature seemed to be in health, although inwardly she was held in an ever stronger grasp, and a consuming fire burnt in her as she walked about her house. Nor did any understand what ailed her, so subtle, hidden and piercing was this divine working. After these days Natural Man was again assailed by new martyrdoms, past curing, which destroyed him. When God tormented the creature's body He strengthened her mind, and when He put her mind to martyrdom He comforted her body; each part of her suffered in its turn. For about ten years she persevered in this state, and every day she understood and knew less of these hidden workings by which God kept her bound to Him.

Afterwards He made her yet more bare outwardly, taking her confessor from her and every other thing to which she could turn her eyes. The Spirit was so eager that it drew all to itself, and this was because it was itself drawn to God by a hidden love (but one without savour), so piercing and great that Spirit, Soul and bodily feelings were melted in it, and all was left sunk in God.

This hidden love stifled, purged and washed away the secret and subtle theft once practised on it, for which penance was thus done secretly, without knowledge of its cause. But Natural Man was left so weighed down and crushed that he could not but say to his Lord in a pitiful voice:

NATURAL MAN: O my God, why hast Thou forsaken

me and left me thus to great outward and inward martyrdom? Yet I may not complain, for even when I suffer all the torment I am able to bear, I am still secretly happy because a subtle and piercing fire of love burns in me, which little by little consumes all my bodily, animal and spiritual strength. It is a wonder to see a creature live who is bereft of strength for living. Outwardly I still feel the loss of my confessor, whom now I hardly see, and I am grown so weak that I no longer have strength to turn to one side or another. And inwardly the hidden strength given me is burning away, so that I no longer feel myself fitted to receive anything from heaven or the earth. I am little more than a dead body; yet must I still live as long as God please. But I know not how I can live without help, and if help were given me I could not receive it.

CHAPTER XI

Of the spark of eternal glory and the strength received from it by the creature. How God drew the Spirit, how it was still busied in God, and of the creature's martyrdom. What it is to live on earth when the Spirit is in heaven. The martyrdom which must be suffered to escape Purgatory.

When this work was nearly ended, God came otherwise to the help of the creature, sometimes shewing her a spark of the glory to which she had already drawn near, now that her soul's affections and her body's feelings had been burnt away. This spark, albeit she saw it for only one instant, so enlivened her inwardly and outwardly that for many days she was strengthened, and it made on her an inward and lasting mark which needed not to be renewed. Then she saw that God kept the Spirit so fixed in Himself that He suffered it not to waver for the least moment of time, and that the more

it was thus busied, the harder it was for it to turn back;
I have indeed no words to tell how it was set against
going back, for it was plunged secretly in a sea which
seemed to it every day to be greater, as God still drew
it into deeper waters. Unceasingly it lost itself and
was changed into God, who spake these words to the
Soul:

THE LORD: My will is that thou meddle no more with
My works, for always thou wouldst steal from them,
making thine own what befits thee not. I will finish
the work without suffering thee to know aught of it;
I will part thee from thy Spirit who shall be drowned
in My abyss.

Natural Man, hearing this, was at his wits' end and
said:

NATURAL MAN: So I am to stay here in torment;
I live not and I cannot die; every day I am more put
upon and all but turned to nothing. When I was shewn
what this busyness is, which is so fixed in God that it
allows not a moment's breathing space, I saw that the
whole weight of it would fall on wretched me, and
so terrible was the thing to me that all my flesh was
afflicted. For to be so fixed, not moving for one instant,
is very well for the blessed in their own country, who
live in God, lost to themselves. But that I should thus
live on earth and the Spirit in heaven is the greatest
wonder ever known, and the most terrible martyrdom
I can suffer in this world.

Then Natural Man was told that whoever would
enter eternal life without passing through Purgatory
must first die to the world while he is alive, so that all
the imperfections of his soul may be burnt away and
it may be swallowed up in God. And God said:

THE LORD: But since I hear thee cry out as thou dost,
I see that thou art not yet dead; indeed thou must still
live until thou attainest to a life which has free course.
When this liveliness of thine has been consumed and thy
feelings have been weakened, thou wilt feel less and wilt

not look forward to thy martyrdom fearfully as now thou dost, but wilt give thyself up to God, not by the powers of thy soul nor by the instinct of thy bodily nature, but because God has taken all the work on Himself.

For God works in us according to His good pleasure, so subtly and secretly that the man in whom the work is done is unaware of it. For man must feel the martyrdom sent him by God, and otherwise would feel it less. For if he were aware of the work he would not cease to steal from God, even against his own will, because of the evil instinct and the bad habits hidden in the most secret part of his soul. But God knows that unless He provide man cannot live in this extremity, and therefore provides for him secretly, in divers ways and at divers times, according to his need. At first God's providence is clearly shewn by signs, but little by little God lessens the number of these signs, as he sees man gain strength for the fight. And the stronger a man is in the beginning, the more may he look to suffer great martyrdom in the end. Verily, God provides for every man according to his need, but what He provides in secret is so great that it cannot be compared with what He provides openly, and until death He never ceases.

END OF PART II OF THE DIALOGUE

PART III

OF QUESTIONS ABOUT GOD'S LOVE FOR MAN WHICH THE
SOUL PUTS TO HER LORD, OF GOD'S LOVING ANSWERS
AND OF HIS LOVE FOR MAN, ALL OF WHICH WAS VERIFIED
IN SAINT CATHERINE.

CHAPTER I

*The Soul asks God what is the cause of His great love
for man who is so set against Him, and what is man
of whom He has such care.*

SOUL: O Lord, I see Thee so much in love with man
that I would know the cause of this great love, the more
because I see that his ways are contrary to Thy will
and strange to Thy love, and that he resists all Thy
works and is ever set against Thee in all things, taken
up by things of the earth, blind, deaf, dumb and mad,
keeping no rule and powerless to do Thy will. Moreover,
Lord, I confess that I know not what man is of whom
I see Thee so careful; hardly can I tell if Thou be his
Lord or his Slave. It is as though love had made Thee
blind and Thou didst not perceive our wretchedness.
I pray Thee, my Lord, to answer me fully about this
thing too.

THE LORD: Thou askest about a thing so great that
thou canst not know it; but to content thine understanding, weak and poor as it is, I will shew thee a spark
of the truth. If I granted thee a clearer vision thou
couldst not live unless My grace sustained thee.

Know first that I am God who change not, and
that I loved man before I created him, with an infinite,
pure, simple and clear love for which there was no
cause, save that I cannot but love what I have created
and ordained to minister, in its degree, to My glory.

And I have provided man richly with all fit means to reach his end, with natural gifts and supernatural graces which he will never lack in so far as they depend on Me; nay more, with My infinite love which by divers ways and means surrounds him so that he may be subject to My care. Only the free will I have given him can be contrary to Me, and against this I never cease to fight, by love, until man gives it to Me, and when I have accepted his gift thereof I make it anew, little by little, working secretly and with loving care. Nor do I ever forsake him until I have brought him to his ordained end.

To thy other question, why I so love this man who sets himself against Me and is so filled with wretchedness that it stinks from earth to heaven, I answer that because of My infinite goodness and the pure love I bear him, I cannot see his faults nor cease to work in him and still to do him good. By My light I shew him his faults so that he may know them, and knowing them may weep, and by tears be cleansed. Know too that I cannot be offended by man save when he hinders the work I have ordained to bring him to his end, that is when My love is prevented from working according to his needs, as it can be only by mortal sin. But thou couldst never understand this love thou seekest to know for it has neither form nor measure. By thine understanding thou canst not know it for it is not to be understood; by its effects it can be known a little, and they are great or small in the measure of man's love which allows them.

Whoever had not lost his faith and saw what I work in men with this spark of love which I put secretly into their hearts, would so burn with love that he could not live, for by the vehemence of this love he would be melted to nothing. Hardly ever does man know this love; and yet for this unknown love's sake men are seen to leave the world, their goods, their friends and their kindred and to hate their other loves and pleasures;

for this love they sell themselves into slavery and are subject to others till they die. So does it grow that they will suffer a thousand martyrdoms for it. This has been tried and seen and is still seen.

Thou mayst see this love turn beasts into men, men into angels, and angels almost into Gods, sharing the Godhead. Thou mayst see men change wholly; from earthly they become heavenly, their souls and bodies practising spiritual things; their speech and their life are changed so that they do and speak against their wont. All who see marvel; the thing seems good to them and almost they are envious, but none understands the work saving him on whom it is wrought. For this inward, piercing and sweet love, which man feels in his heart, is unknown, nor can it be known or told or understood save with the understanding of the affections. With that understanding man knows himself to be busied, bound, changed, content, at peace and ordered, his bodily feelings consenting. He has nothing, would have nothing, is fain for nothing; he is quiet, satisfied in his inmost heart, aware of nought else. He is closely bound by the finest thread secretly held in My hand, who let man fight and withstand the world, the demons and himself, seeing himself the while most weak and utterly without help, so that he fears at any moment to fall. But I suffer him not to fall.

Even this, O Soul, is not that true love which thou seekest to understand. That love comes when, by all means fitted to man's wretchedness, I have burnt away his imperfections, outward and inward. Other work I do unseen: with the finest golden thread, which is My hidden love, I come down to man, and to the thread a hook is fixed which catches his heart. He feels the wound but knows not who has caught and tied him; he cannot and would not move, for it is I, his object and his end, who draw the thread, but this he understands not. I, however, who hold the thread in My hand, still draw him to Me with a love so fine and piercing that he is overcome and conquered and rapt from himself.

As a man on the gallows touches not the earth with his feet but hangs in mid air by the rope which kills him, so also this spirit hangs by the thread of this finest love which kills all man's hidden, lurking and unknown imperfections. And all that he loves thereafter he loves with the love of this thread which he feels binding his heart. So also are all his other works wrought by this love, and by grace they are made acceptable to me. It is I who work of My pure love; man meddles not in it. I, having taken this man into My care and drawn him to Myself, work thus, and enrich him with My benefits, so increasing them that at the hour of his death he is drawn by the thread of love and drowned unawares in the divine abyss. And though man, in the state of which I have spoken, seems a thing dead, lost and abject, he has nevertheless found his life, hidden in Me, in whom are all the treasures and riches of eternal life. Nor can that be told or thought which I have prepared for My beloved soul.

Hearing these things, the Soul, on fire and burning with love, could not do other than say:

CHAPTER II

The Soul's exclamations. Our Lord asks her what has dulled her. Of the taste she has got for the company of spiritual persons and of the pleasant colloquies among them.

SOUL: O tongue, why speakest thou who findest no words proper to the love my heart feels? O heart on fire with love, why dost thou not burn away the body which holds thee? O spirit, what dost thou, still tied here to the earth? Seest thou not the vehemence of the love with which God draws thee and longs for thee? Break this body in pieces so that body and spirit may go each to its own place!

God, seeing the Soul thus ablaze beyond all measure, and wishing to stay her a little, shewed her a spark of the love with which He loves man, and this love is so pure, simple and clean that the Soul, seeing it, was amazed, astonied and as though forsaken within herself. Then our Lord called her and said:

THE LORD: What ails thee? Why art thou so changed? What new thing hast thou seen and what has stayed thee, on fire with love as thou wast? Once it seemed that thou must break thy body in pieces to get the object of thy love, so great was the delight, so grateful the savour you knew, thou and many friends of thine to whom thou wast joined in the bonds of this gentle and sweet love. And now I see thee strayed and forsaken, and as though thou wouldst no longer know any man.

In times past indeed, this Soul was often with her spiritual friends, and they spoke of the divine love in such wise that it seemed to all and each of them they were already in Paradise. What pleasant colloquies there were! Both he who spoke and he who listened were fed by sweet and delightful spiritual food. Time flew too fast; they could not have their fill; they were so much on fire, so ablaze, that often they could not speak, nor could they part from one another; they seemed to be rapt from themselves. O what feasts of love! What grateful viands! What gracious union! What divine companionship! They talked only of the divine love, its workings and how to dispel any hindrance to it. Clearly, all that passed between them was for God and the profit of souls; none could think otherwise.

But the Soul, answering the Lord, said:

CHAPTER III

The Soul acknowledges that what she seemed to do for God came of self-love. She is left amazed by her sight of pure love and asks what is this love. Our Lord answers her that she cannot understand it, for He who is love can be understood only by His effects.

SOUL: Lord, Thou hast shewn me a new light by which I have seen that all that other love of mine was self-love; my works which seemed to me filled with love of Thee, and done for Thee, were all defiled by self, for they all passed through me and secretly I took them for mine own; they stayed hidden in me, beneath Thy shadow, O Lord, in whom I rested. But since I have seen Thy love, pure, simple, clean and burning, and its workings, I have been taken out of myself and as though dead to myself, and my other loves, so much my own, have gone out of me. O love divine, what can I ever again say of thee? I am overcome and conquered by thee; I feel that I die of love, yet feel no love; I am drowned in love and know not love; I feel this love working in me and understand not what it does; I feel my heart burning with love and see not the fire.

O my Lord, I cannot stay from seeking some notion of this love, and albeit utterly conquered by the new light Thou hast shewn me, still I despair not of knowing more of this love. It holds all that is to be desired in heaven and on earth. It contents man, yet never satiates him; nay rather, it sharpens his hunger unceasingly. So sweet and pleasant, so suited to the heart of man, is this pure love, that whoever has tasted one particle of it can never more cease to follow after it, though he should leave his bodily life a thousand times over. What is this love which conquers all? Lord, Thou hast told me much of it, yet still I seem not to have heard enough, and since Thou hast given me a burning instinct to seek more knowledge, I have faith that my quest is not vain. Thou hast promised me some satisfaction and I am not yet satisfied. A spark of Thy pure love Thou hast shewn me, and it has lit in my heart a fire which consumes me. I neither find a place on earth in which to rest, nor see or feel aught but this love; I am rapt from myself and amazed and know not where I am; I am seized and caught and wounded almost to death, awaiting only what Thou shalt provide to satisfy every desire ordained in me.

THE LORD: O my beloved Soul, thou seekest to know what thou canst not understand. Thy instinct and thy desire are, in respect of man still in the flesh, supernatural, but in respect of what is spiritual and the end for which thou wast created, they are natural, for love has been thy beginning and thy mean and must be thy end; and seeing that love is thy life in this world and the next, thou canst not live without it. Therefore art thou on fire with desire to know what this love is, but thou canst know it neither by thy understanding, nor by thy spirit, nor by any love thou thyself feelest. For even they who are already in their true home understand it only in the measure of the grace and the charity they have had in this life.

For it is I God who am love, who can be understood only by the effects of this great love, such as I have shewn and unceasingly shew them to be, and such that their worth is beyond thought or reckoning. When I let a soul see a spark of My simple and pure love, it is constrained to give it back to Me, for such is its strength that it forces the soul to do for me all it can, even to suffer not one but a thousand deaths, if that could be, and infinite martyrdoms. How great the love is which is poured into the hearts of men can be seen by its effects, that is by their works wrought for love of Me. But I see, beloved Soul, that thou seekest not to know this active love by its effects, but art in quest of the sweet drop of love which I instil in the hearts of my elect and which melts in them soul and spirit and bodily feelings, so that they can no longer move of themselves. This drop plunges the soul in the sweetness of love, so that it can do nothing and stays lost in itself and strange to everything created, while the creature in his inmost heart is content and at peace with all. There is nought for him to do, for by this drop of love which satisfies him, albeit he is not fed, he is busied.

Then this Soul of whom I speak was set on fire and cried:

SOUL: O food without savour! O savour without taste! O taste without meat! O meat of love by which angels, saints and men are fed! O beatific food! He who tastes thee knows little what has come to him. O meat which truly appeases our hunger! Thou quenchest all other appetites. Who tastes this food deems himself blessed even in this life, in which God shews him only one little morsel of it, for if we saw more he would die of this subtle and piercing love; the spirit would burn so that the weak body would be consumed. O heavenly love! O love divine! Thou hast shut up my mouth; I cannot speak for I know not how. No longer will I seek what cannot be found. I am conquered and overcome.

CHAPTER IV

Who finds the love of God is he whose heart is clean. How that love works in secret and subtly, doing nothing outwardly. Of certain of its effects. Of the Soul's exclamations on this love and of its properties.

THE LORD: O beloved Soul, knowest thou who finds My love? He who has cleansed his heart and rid it of all other love. And when he has found it he is content and satisfied, albeit he knows neither My way of working nor his own state, for love works in secret and subtly, doing nothing outwardly.

This man is ever busied though he has no business; he is bound and knows not who holds him; he is in a prison without a door. He can use neither understanding, memory nor will and seems to be insensible, dumb and blind, for divine love has overcome and bound all the feelings of his soul and body. Therefore this soul and spirit, feeling themselves turned from their wonted love and works and drawn by a higher and stronger working, are driven to say:

O Lord, what is this that love is doing? What is this love which works so great a change in man, from good still to better, which leads him unceasingly onward and nearer his last end? How comes it that the more he goes forward, the less he understands and the more he wonders, not knowing where he is?

This man lives by the arrows of love which God shoots into his heart and which are borne back to heaven on burning sighs; without this much refreshment he could not live, so vehement is the fire of love. Some-times, to hasten its work, this love so constrains him that he has leave neither to speak nor to sigh. However, he is not kept thus long for he could not bear it and live.

Then the enlightened Soul, on fire with divine love and filled with sweetness and pleasantness, cried out:

SOUL: O love, for the heart which tastes thee eternal life begins in this world! Lord, Thou hidest this working from him in whom Thou accomplishest it, lest he spoil Thy work by something of self. O love, he who feels thee understands thee not, and he who would under-stand thee cannot know thee. O love, our life, our blessedness, our rest! Divine love brings with it every good and chases away all evil. O heart wounded by divine love, thou art past curing; done to death by this sweet wound, thou livest again with an infinite life. O fire of love, what workest thou in this man? Thou purifiest him as fire purifies gold; then thou leadest him with thee to that end for which thou hast created him.

Love is a divine flame, and even as material fire ever warms, working according to its nature, so God's love, by its nature, works in man and raises him to his end, nor rests from working for his benefit and profit, for God is ever man's lover. He who feels not this love is himself to blame, for while man is in this life God never turns from doing good to him and ever loves him.

O love, I cannot hold my peace, yet cannot speak as I would of thy sweet and pleasant working. Every part of me is filled with thee, so that I am moved to speak, and yet I cannot. Alone, within myself, I speak with my heart and mind, but when I would find words to say what I feel, I am prevented, for my weak tongue fails me. Then I would be still, yet cannot, for an instinct urges me to speak. If I could speak of this love which I feel in my heart, I think every other heart would catch fire, however far from love it might be. If but, before I left this life, I might once speak of it as I would, as I feel it in me and as it works in me! If but I might tell what it asks of man into whom it pours itself and whom it fills, so that no part of him is empty of a sweetness passing all others and a contentment which cannot be told! By this love man would let himself be burnt alive, for God joins to it a zeal by which man makes nothing of any obstacle, however great.

O love, mighty and sweet, blessed is he whom thou ownest. Thou strengthenest him, thou defendest and preservest him against everything contrary to thee in his soul or body. Thou leadest all things gently to their end, nor ever forsakest man. Thou art faithful to him; thou givest him light to see the wiles of the devil, the wickedness of the world, and himself who is filled with selfishness and perversity. So efficacious art thou, so enlightening, that thou drawest all the imperfections out of our hidden and secret depths, and placest them before our eyes that we may mend them and cleanse ourselves of them.

This love leads and governs our will that it may be strong and never fail, and may fight against temptation, and it busies the affections and the understanding so that they seek nothing else. Memory is absorbed by it, and the powers of the soul are satisfied so that love alone dwells in the soul and owns it, letting none other enter therein. Love ever bears in itself a sweet savour by which man suffers himself to be guided; so pleasant it is, that even if he reach salvation by way of many torments, there is no martyrdom which he endures not willingly.

O love, though I speak of thee I cannot tell the sweetness and gentleness thou bringest to my heart; thou art in my heart and as I speak of thee thou blazest forth. To one who hears or reads these words and feels no love, thou seemest of little account; words pass him like the wind, leaving no savour. But if I could tell the joy, the happiness, the contentment which this love gives to the heart of the beloved, all men who heard or read these words would be taken captive, nor ever resist, for the human heart no sooner feels this love, which is suited to it, than it opens to be filled, albeit none can be filled with divine love who has not first rid himself of all other love. And when the heart feels even the least drop of this love, it so thirsts for more that it counts all else it might desire in this world as nothing. By this love man fights the evil habits which hold him back from getting it; by this holy love he is made ever ready for any great work.

CHAPTER V

Other effects of love. How it works when it will, and how its work is all its own. Of the works of love, in love and by love, and their explanation.

O love, by thy sweetness thou breakest hearts harder than diamonds and meltest them like wax in the fire! O love, thou causest the great to deem themselves the meanest on earth and the rich the poorest of the world! O love, wise men thou makest to seem foolish, and takest their learning from the learned, giving them a knowledge which passes all understanding! O love, thou drivest all sadness from the heart, and all hardness, all selfishness, all worldly delight! Thou art cunning to seize man of his own free will, so that he is content to be guided by thee alone, for thou art our guide.

O love, thy works are strange to the earth, for from earthly thou makest man heavenly and unskilled in worldly works, taking from him all means of busying himself on earth! O love, thine are all the deeds of our salvation, for we cannot do them without thee nor know we how! O love, so pleasant is thy name that it sweetens all things; pleasant are the lips which name thee, above all when one speaks from a heart filled with the great sweetness which flows from thee, and which renders a man benign, mild, gracious, merry, liberal, ready to serve all men as much as he can. O love, when thy gentle and gracious dart can find a way to pierce man's heart, and it is at leisure and not filled with another love, then, however small be the spark thou lightest, he leaves all for thee.

This love makes every bitterness and hindrance seem sweet. O love, what sweet pleasantness and pleasant sweetness thou bringest with thee! All have thee in common; the greater the number of the creatures into whom thou pourest thyself, the more is thy will done, the more man feels and knows thy pleasant fire, and the more he burns with it and longs for it. He asks no other proof than what he feels; he can give no other reason; love takes away reason and will and is left master of the whole man. Love does what it will with him, as and when it will; all he does is love's work, for now all his works are done through love or in love or by love.

A man's works are wrought through love when he does all for the love of God, which God has given him together with the instinct to work for his own profit or that of his neighbour. In this first state of love God causes a man to do, with pious affection, many profitable and necessary works. The works of the second state of love are wrought in God, and are those a man does without looking to his profit or that of his neighbour; these works are ever in God and are done without object, man persevering in them because he has the habit of them, and God having taken from him his own share in the business which used to help and delight him. They are more perfect than the works of the first state which had many objects grateful to the soul and body. The works done by love are more perfect than those of these two states, because man has no part in them at all, for love has so overcome and conquered him that he is drowned in the sea of love, nor knows where he is; he is lost to himself and can do nothing of himself. Here it is love itself which works in man, and these are the works of perfection for man has no part in them. They are the works of grace, *gratum facientes*, which are wholly acceptable to God.

This sweet and pure love has laid hold on man and drawn him to itself, stripping him of his own self of which it has taken possession. Unceasingly it works in him, only for his benefit and profit, without his meddling in the matter.

O love, how sweet is thy company and how faithful

thy guidance! Never can one say, never can one think, enough good of thee! Blessed is the heart thou ownest and imprisonest! Love makes men just, simple, pure, rich, wise and happy, and tempers all bitterness with its sweetness.

O love, all that is done through thee is done easily, cheerfully and willingly. Weariness is manifold but thy sweetness lightens all effort. O what torment it is to work without love! Who could measure that torment? Love gives sweet savour to every food, makes it good if it be bad and better if it be good. God pours into the heart of man as much love as it can hold, according to its degree.

How sweet it would be to speak of this love, could words be found proper to the sweetness it brings to man's heart! But because the soul is immortal and fit for more love than it can feel in this life (the body being too weak to bear all the love for which the soul is fain), therefore it still longs and hungers for what it lacks, nor can it ever be wholly at rest in this life.

O love, thou fillest man's heart but art too great for him to understand; he is left happy but not satisfied. Through the heart thou wholly seizest and holdest a man, so that he lets none but thee come in, and thou bindest with strong bonds all the feelings of his soul and body. O sweet slavery of love which makes man free, in this world most happy and in the next everlastingly blessed!

O love, thy bonds are so gentle and strong that they bind the angels and the saints together; they are firm and close and never break. Men linked by this chain are so united that they have but one will and one object, and all things temporal and spiritual seem to be owned by them in common. Within these bonds there is no difference between rich and poor, between nation and nation. All contrariness ceases where there is this love; it straightens what is crooked and brings contraries together.

CHAPTER VI

The Soul puts divers questions to Our Lord. How the martyrs suffered through this love. How charity is the shortest and surest road to salvation; without it the soul would cast itself into a thousand hells rather than enter God's presence.

O my Love, sweet Jesus, what made Thee come from heaven to earth?

Love.

What made Thee suffer such great and terrible torments even to death?

Love.

What made Thee leave Thyself as food for the soul?

Love.

What moved Thee, and moves Thee still, to send the Holy Ghost to be our strength and our guide?

Love.

Many more things might be said of Thee. Only for love, Thou camest into this world in so vile and mean an outward seeming, and didst so humble Thyself before the people, that not only wast Thou not acknowledged God, Thou wast hardly taken for a man. No servant, however faithful and loving, would bear as much for his master, even if he were promised Paradise, for without the inward love Thou givest no torment of soul or body can be borne patiently.[1]

But Thou, Lord, didst bring from heaven this pleasant manna and sweet food, giving strength by which any suffering can be borne, as we know because this has been proved first by Thee, our sweet Master, and then by Thy saints. O what things Thy love, poured into

[1] The author, absorbed by the beauty of her vision, forgets the suffering and death often patiently borne by unbelievers for a master or cause, in her time and before it as in ours.

Thy saints' hearts, caused them very patiently to do and bear! They were on fire with this love, so that they stayed united to Thee and no torment could separate them from Thee. For as they suffered, a zeal was kindled in them which grew with their pains, and therefore no martyrdom invented by the most cruel tyrants could overcome them, and they were vainly tortured by men who looked only to the weakness of their flesh, seeing neither the sweet and strong love· nor the zeal which God had put in their hearts, which zeal has such live-liness and might that whoever holds it fast can never perish.

No shorter, better and surer way to salvation can be found than to put on the sweet wedding garment of charity, which gives the soul such confidence and strength that it enters God's presence without fear. But if, at the time of death, the soul be bare of charity, it is left so mean and vile that rather than appear in the divine presence it would go to any other place, however sad and evil. For God, who is simple and pure, can receive nothing into Himself but pure and simple love. Since God is a sea of love, in which all the saints are drowned and sunk, the least imperfec-tion cannot enter into Him. Therefore the soul bare of charity, who is separated from the body and thus understands these truths, would cast itself into hell rather than come before this purity and simplicity.

O pure love, the least stain made by a fault is to thee a great hell, more terrible, so vehement art thou, than the hell of the damned! But this will be neither believed nor understood by any not skilled and prac-tised in thee. One can speak of this love, as indeed I now do, infinite though it be, because in its beloved soul it works in a gracious and familiar way, as though it were one and the same thing as this soul.

CHAPTER VII

*Our Lord questions the Soul about the love she feels and
the words Love says to her. She answers as best she can,
but cannot tell what she feels or how she burns with love.
She asks Our Lord how a soul in love with Him can live
on earth and in what conditions.*

THE LORD: What then wouldst thou say, O Soul,
of this Love, thy beloved, who never leaves thee? He
still speaks to thee, comforts thee, sets thee on fire, shews
thee ever more heavenly beauty to kindle further the
affection thou bearest him. Tell Me now some of the
loving words he says to thee when thou art alone and
thinkest on him.

SOUL: I hear words of love spoken to me which I
understand in my inmost heart and which set it on fire.
I know not how to tell these words or this feeling of love,
nor can I tell them for the words are not like others.
This love opens my heart and pours into it news so
gracious that all within it is on fire and burnt away.
I cannot tell the words one by one, nor tell of that fire
and love. My heart is seized, busied, held by loving
contentment.

The Soul understood not how the work was done,
yet understood that love, thus visiting a beloved soul,
bestowed on it every imaginable caress which one true
friend could ever give another, however great the love
between them. Thus love melted this Soul, lifted her up
from the earth, purified, simplified, comforted and
strengthened her, drawing her ever deeper and deeper
into its furnace. It suffered her not to stay long in this
piercing and great fire, for mankind could not long
bear such vehemence of love. But an imprint was left
on the creature's heart so that, by love, she lived almost
always in God.

SOUL: O love, thou didst take this heart into thyself and left Natural Man forsaken on earth, where he found neither a place nor rest for himself. He was like one in exile, for no object for life was left to him in heaven or on earth.

O love, who wast so much on fire with love for this Soul in which thou didst work lovingly, I would know how this creature lived on earth, soul and body, and how she found herself there. What was her converse in heaven and with creatures on the earth? I know that she led a life very different from that of others, one admirable rather than edifying. She counted nothing of any worth; poor though she was, she seemed to be lady of heaven and mistress of the earth. Few understood her. She had great freedom and no fear of ever lacking anything; she had nothing and yet seemed to own everything.

THE LORD: My answer is not for blind men without the divine light, whose minds are so busied with earthly things that they cannot understand My words, but for the few who, having my divine light, will understand. As for this Soul, My love so delighted her that it consumed in her all other delights a man could have in this world, for to taste of Me quenches every other taste and My light blinds whoever sees it. All the feelings of this Soul were so seized by this love and bound up in it that she knew neither where nor what she was, neither what she had done nor what she should do. She was, as it were, beside herself, without reason or memory or will.

Creatures who are thus have no taste left them; they no longer delight in the things of the world but use them only as they must, and they take what they must without pleasure, almost as they would a medicine. They are ever busied within themselves and this busyness takes from them all appetite for temporal food. God sends flames and burning and subtle darts of love which pierce their inmost hearts, and the man on whom these come is like one lost, not knowing where he is. But inwardly he is held within this close and most subtle love. In it his soul is plunged; it is dumb; it knows not how to speak and cannot speak, and if God did not soon withdraw Himself and His strong love, it would depart from the body. Yet God, in withdrawing Himself, leaves so sweet a busyness to the soul that it would see, taste or hear of nothing else. This man marvels that any should have in mind aught else than what he feels. Until the imprint made on his soul has grown fainter, he can give no thought to worldly business, however necessary.

CHAPTER VIII

The condition of the Soul in love with love. How God delays to give her knowledge of her faults because she could not bear it. When she has any suspicion of a fault in herself she has no rest until her spirit has made satisfaction.

This was the condition of the loving Soul. So delicate was her conscience that she could not bear to harbour even a slight suspicion of a fault in herself, since love cannot dwell with the least imperfection; nay, rather than suspect a fault in herself this Soul in love would all but have endured the pains of hell. And since man cannot stay in this life and not commit faults, God sometimes kept her ignorant of hers, because she could not bear them, and at another time gave her knowledge of every fault she had; thus He cleansed her.

If suspicion of a fault in herself came to this Soul, she had no rest nor peace until her mind was satisfied. This Soul, living in that loving peace, could not bear to be troubled, either within herself or in her relations with others. And if any were troubled because of her,

she was not at peace until she had made satisfaction
as best she could. When minds thus used to the divine
love are for some reason troubled (by God's leave),
they are all but unbearable to themselves; for they are
outside the quiet paradise in which they are used to
dwell, and if God did not restore them to their wonted
state they would hardly be able to live. These creatures
live in great freedom and make little account of earthly
things. Nearly always they are rapt from themselves,
especially as they near the term of this life, for they
are bare of what belongs to it, plunged in that love
by whose gracious working they had learnt that God
has taken change of them, soul and body, and suffers
them to lack nothing.

The Lord shewed this Soul too that all the good,
whether spiritual or temporal, which these creatures
have from others comes to them because these others
are moved by God. So clearly did the Soul see this
that she could be grateful to no creature for any benefit,
knowing that the thing was God's work and provided
by Him. This vision set her ever more and more on
fire until she was made nothing, and then at last she
gave herself up wholly to that love, letting all creatures
go. And God satisfied her so that she saw only love
and made no count of aught else.

And if it seem to thee that creatures who are thus
have any affection for outward things, take heed lest
thou believe it. Rather think it impossible that any
love but the love of God can enter into their minds,
unless indeed the Lord suffer it because of a need of
the soul or the body. But the love and care therefore
given is no hindrance to them, for it does not touch
their inmost hearts but only meets the need ordained
by God. Pure love must be free from subjection, inward
or outward, for where the Spirit of God is, there is
liberty.

O, who will perceive this sweet intercourse? Who
will hear these burning words? This joyous ardour

in which neither God nor man is discerned, so little at leisure is the heart! It is as though God sent His beloved souls a little paradise to be a sample of the great and true one. He is prodigal of His love tokens, known only to His lovers who are sunk and drowned in the sea of divine love.

O love, the heart that is thine is so magnanimous and the mind so great that the creature would accept most painful martyrdom with that peace he enjoys, rather than any good thing on earth or in heaven without it; but none knows the worth of that peace who does not feel and taste it. The heart that is in God sees all created things as beneath it, not out of pride or haughtiness but because of the union wrought between it and God, which makes all that is of God seem to this heart to be its own. Saving God it neither sees nor knows nor understands anything. A heart in love with God cannot be defeated, for God is its strength, nor can it fear hell or have joy in paradise. It is so ordered that it takes all that comes to it from God's hand. With Him it dwells at peace about all things. A man whose heart is in God can hardly be moved by his neighbours, so ordered and strengthened is he within himself by God.

SOUL: O love, how dost thou call these souls who are dear to thee?

THE LORD: *Ego dixi Dii estis, et filii excelsi omnes.*

SOUL: O love, thou bringest thy lovers to be nothing in themselves; then in thyself thou makest them anew and free, with a true and perfect freedom which is in thee; yet thou leavest them still masters of themselves. They will only what God wills; all else is grave hindrance to them.

O love, I find no words meet to declare how kind and pleasant is thy yoke or how strong and sure thy freedom or how sweet thy gentle graciousness. Whatever the true lover says and can say of love, never will he be able to declare it as he would. He seeks for loving words proper to this love and never finds them, for love and its works are infinite and our tongue not only finite but most weak. Never can the lover satisfy himself; he is left confused, unable to find words for what he is fain to say. But although what can be told is almost nothing, yet man refreshes himself a little by speaking of what his heart feels, so that he does not die of love. And Thou, Lord, what sayest Thou of this Thy beloved Soul?

THE LORD: I say that she is all mine. And thou, Soul, what sayest thou of thy love?

SOUL: I say that my God is wounded with love and that in this love I live joyful and content.

CHAPTER IX

Of the condition of the Body. How Natural Man lived in torment and like one dead, and how God provided for him. Of the Soul's happiness when she could love and love again, and how, bereft of this happiness, she was left as though dead.

Now that the condition of the Soul on fire and ablaze with divine love has been shewn, there is something to be said of the condition of her Body. The body cannot live on love as the soul can, but lives on material food. And since God willed to cut this Soul off from worldly things and her Body, and to draw her wholly to spiritual works, this Body was left without strength and almost without food, for the link between the Soul and the Body had been taken away, and without it the Body had no strength but was almost as the Soul was when she was without God, that is like a dead thing. If God had kept the Soul long in His vehement grasp, the Body could by his nature not have lived. God, who sees all things and provides for all according to their needs, left Natural Man with little comfort, so that he neither smiled, nor tasted food, nor slept, nor could he take delight in the feeling of the Soul or the Body or in worldly things, saving in that little which God granted him to sustain his life of travail.

That ever imperfection which lives in man may die in God while he still lives on earth, God, as it were, trips up natural man, and the soul too, as though into a bath, and cuts him, and when no blood is left in the body and the soul is all in God, then each goes to its own place; that is, the soul stays in God and the body goes to the grave. And this work is done by love only and secretly. If you knew how pressed upon is Natural Man and how besieged, you would in truth deem that no creature on earth could so suffer. But because the thing is not seen it is not believed nor understood and wakens no pity, the less because these sufferings are borne for the love of God. Whatever the suffering, I say that the creature must, for the love of God, still live like one dead. The creature is like a man hung up by his feet and living thus; even thus his heart may be happy, but what good can his body enjoy?

Thus it was with this Natural Man: he could not live naturally; I see him as though he were ever crucified and greatly afflicted. He lived and knew not on what food or how; he desired nothing but lived in God. Often, moreover, God sent to the heart He loved so many sharp arrows of fire that it seemed as though the Body must be melted by the ardour of this loving and piercing fire, which brought the Soul to a dark and secret happiness of which she fain would never have been rid, for in it she found the blessedness and rest natural to her. This happiness God often shews to the hearts He loves.

But the Body, being constrained to follow the Soul (for since the body is not spirit it can neither live nor do anything else without the soul), this Body, I say, was left meanwhile as though he had no soul, without any comfort and as weak as though he were dead. He could not help himself, not knowing how, and therefore others had to help him unless God provided for him secretly. Otherwise the creature would have been forlorn as a little child who has had all he needs taken from him, and can but weep until he is given what he needs. It is not then to be marvelled at that God provides for such creatures certain men who help them, and by means of whom their souls and bodies are succoured, for otherwise they could not live. See how Our Lord Jesus Christ left Saint John to His beloved Mother to cherish her, and He did as much for His disciples. And He still does as much for those who are devoted to Him, so that, being divinely united, one succours another in soul and in body. And since most men are ignorant of these workings and have not this union one with another, there needs must be certain men through whom God works by His grace and His light.

He who sees the creatures of whom I speak and knows them not will rather wonder at them than be edified by them. Beware then of judging them lest you fall into error.

Consider now in what straits and subjection this Natural Man was placed when he lived, as it were, without life. He lived because God kept him alive, by grace; he could not live naturally. When the Soul could love and love yet again, a savour by which Natural Man lived was still left to her, but when this active and passive love was taken from her, then Natural Man was weak and forlorn, almost as though dead. Then God once more worked subtly and secretly in the Soul, and this work of love was nobler and more perfect than that which had been done before God had stripped the Soul and made her naked. No food at all was left to the Soul, but in the strength of God she stood firm and established.

CHAPTER X

How the soul, the heart and the spirit of this creature were emptied of all forms, and were held in a way which through them cannot be known. How her heart was made the tabernacle of God into which many graces and much sweetness were shed, such as bore admirable fruit. How few are the creatures led along this road. Of the nakedness of the spirit and its union with God.

THE LORD: What wilt thou do, O Soul, who art thus naked and bereft? What will ye do, O heart and mind, who are thus emptied? How is it that ye are in this state of which ye know nothing?

SOUL: I no longer know where I am; I have lost will, knowledge, memory and love and all taste for anything; I cannot account for myself; I cannot see where I am; I can neither seek nor find anything at all.

This creature's heart and mind, being empty of all the forms through which paradise once seemed to come to her, now said:

We are held in a grasp so hidden and subtle that we cannot make it known. But in that which holds us a loving and most subtle spirit is contained and concentrated, and the creature is filled with it so that her soul, her heart, her mind and her body, and her bones, sinews and blood, seem to overflow with it; her whole being is held in this love by her hidden thoughts; every sigh her heart breathes comes from a fire which rages in her secretly. But the body, which cannot bear such mighty heat in silence, laments. This creature's mouth is filled with burning arrows and loving thoughts which come from her heart; it seems that such words of piercing love as would break a heart of iron must issue from her lips; yet she cannot say what she would, for her true and loving converse, of which the sweetness passes thought, is inward. Her heart has been made the tabernacle of God, into which He pours, for itself and others, many graces which secretly bear admirable fruits. This creature carries heaven within herself in secret.

If such creatures (who are rare in this world) were known, they would be worshipped on earth. But God keeps them unknown to themselves and others until the time of their death when the true is known from the false. O how few creatures are led along this road of subtle and piercing love, which so constrains the soul and the body that it leaves in them no imperfection, since none, however slight, can be borne by pure love! Love's secret working perseveres in the soul until it has cleansed it wholly, so as to lead it to its end without any purgatory.

O soul, O heart, O mind, enclosed and imprisoned in this divine fire! If any could understand the beauty, the wisdom and the loving care which God, of His love, has shed in you, and His gentle, pleasant and gracious converse with you, his heart would be melted however hard it were.

O love, we call thee so until all the love poured by God into man's heart be consumed; thereafter man is so drunk with love, so sunk in it, that he no longer knows what love is. For this love then becomes spirit, and is joined to man's spirit so that he becomes spiritual; and since spirit is invisible and cannot be discerned by the powers of the soul, man is conquered and overcome so that he no longer knows where he is, nor where he should halt nor whither he should go. By this hidden and intimate union with God in the spirit, such sweetness is imprinted and such strong contentment established in the soul that no martyrdom could undo them. The soul has a zeal so ardent that if a man had a thousand lives he would risk them all to conform to this inward imprint, of which the power is such that hell cannot appal it.

O naked and invisible spirit, so bare art thou that none can hold thee back. Thy dwelling is in heaven albeit in the body thou art still on earth. Thou neither knowest thyself nor art known to others in this world. All thy friends and thy kindred are in heaven and known to thee alone, by an inward instinct which the Spirit of God gives thee.

O could I but find meet words to expound this gracious friendship and this lost union! Lost, I say, as to man's part in it, for he has lost all the words for this love and union, this nothingness which comes on him, this change, sweetness, gentleness, kindness. He has indeed lost the words which would expound the union of two separate things so that they are made one naked spirit, active beyond measure; it is a thing not to be understood.

CHAPTER XI

Of the secret means God uses to purify man. Of His loving care for man. How out of love, not wishing him to work for his own profit, He sweetly deceives him. How the true nakedness of the spirit cannot be told in words.

O my sweet Lord, how many secret means Thou usest to work in man when Thou wouldst purify him by Thy love, which takes all rust away from the soul and makes it fit for most holy union with Thee! O great and pleasant country, unknown to unhappy mortals, for which mortal men have been created by God!

O infinite Good, how can it be that Thou art not loved and known by him who has been granted the power to know and enjoy Thee, if but through that slight feeling and taste which God gives, of His grace? Even in this world man should leave all things else to have Thee.

O Lord, what loving care Thou hast, by day and night, of man who knows not himself and knows Thee even

less, greatly though Thou lovest him most diligently
though Thou seekest him, and patiently though Thou
bearest with and awaitest him, of Thy divine love!

Thou art that most great and high God of whom none
can speak or think, so unutterably supreme are Thy
greatness, Thy might, Thy wisdom and Thy infinite
goodness. And all these things Thou usest for this vile
man whom Thou wouldst render great and worthy.
To this end dost Thou, for love of him, still deceive
him, not willing, because of the free will Thou hast
given him, to constrain him. By love Thou drawest
men to Thee, and Thy will is that they yield to Thee
out of love. With Thy love Thou workest in and by
them, and Thy will is that with love they work with
all their powers, for without love nothing good is done.
Thou workest only for man's profit, and wouldst have
man work not for his own profit but only for Thine
honour. Thou who art God and Lord hast not looked
to Thine own ease nor to that of Thy soul or body in
order to save man, and Thou willest that neither should
he look to the ease of his soul or body when he has to do
Thy will. Thy will is all for our profit, although man,
wretched and blind, knows it not.

In speaking of this naked spirit I have departed from
my matter. This is because there are no words to shew
its true nakedness; when the soul is naked it has a fullness
of understanding which is beyond words, and yet because
of the vehemence which has seized it and which man
feels in himself, he is forced to speak, using the fittest
words he can. To use them is like writing with black
and ill-smelling ink; yet by this means or some other
many notions are understood which would not otherwise
be known.

Ah me, if man could understand what the mind in
this state knows, these words would indeed seem black
and ill smelling to him! What then will those hearts
and tongues do which cannot tell these notions? So
secret are they and so hidden that he who has them

thinks that none will be found to understand them
and that he cannot tell them. Shall he then stay silent
and astonied? No, for it seems to him that he cannot
hold his peace; more and more is his heart set on fire
by the admirable and loving work which, day by day,
he sees God accomplish in him, more and more, and
which binds him so tight with an invisible cord of love
that his nature can hardly bear it, the less when he sees
his fellow men so madly taken up by outward things
that they neither understand nor foresee nor know this
so necessary work. But God so loves us that, albeit He
sees us thus blind and deaf to our good, He ceases not to
knock at our hearts with good inspirations, so that He
may enter into our hearts and make them a tabernacle
into which no created thing can ever enter more.

CHAPTER XII

*The Soul exclaims on the hindrances the creature puts in the
way of God's love. Of God's secret working in man, to
awaken him and make him aware by love. The Soul asks how
man is thus moved and what are grace and the ray of love.*

Ah me, how few and seldom found are the creatures
in whom God dwells, thus working in them! O God,
Thou keepest Thy love in Thyself because Thou canst
not shed it on Thy creatures, so held are they to the earth
by earthly business.

O earth, earth, what wilt thou make of these men
whom thou drawest into thyself? The soul lost, the
body corrupted: all will be lost in torment unending
and unutterable. Think, think on that, O Soul, and take
heed henceforth lest thou waste this time thou now hast
and the means of escaping so many perils. Now God
is kind and propitious to thee, very careful of thy salvation; He seeks and calls thee with unmeasured love.

The works which God does for us unceasingly are such and so many that they cannot be told or thought, but all the good God has done, does, will do and would have done for us will turn to our judgment and confusion if we be lacking, unwilling to work for Him rightly in this time of unknown span.

SOUL: O my Lord, tell me, if it please Thee, how Thou workest within man through Thy hidden love by which he is caught, not knowing what has caught him or how, so that, with a contented mind, he finds himself imprisoned by love.

THE LORD: With my love I move the heart of man, and moving it give him a light by which to know that I inspire him to do well; in this light he ceases his ill-doing and fights against his evil concupiscence.

SOUL: What is this moving? And how comes it to man who neither knows it nor asks for it?

THE LORD: The pure, clear and great love I bear him moves Me to do him the grace of knocking at his heart to see if he will open to Me and let me enter in, that I may make his heart My dwelling-place and drive all else away.

SOUL: What is this grace?

THE LORD: It is an inspiration which I send him by means of a ray of love and by which I grant him the instinct to love, and he cannot do other than love albeit he knows not what. But little by little he comes to know.

SOUL: What is this ray of love?

THE LORD: See the rays of the sun: so subtle and piercing are they that human eyes cannot look at them without losing their sight. Such are the rays of My love which I send into men's hearts, and which cause them to lose their taste and sight for all worldly things.

SOUL: How come these rays into men's hearts?

THE LORD: Like arrows aimed now at one and now at another: in secret they touch the heart, set it on fire and bring forth sighs from it. And man knows not what is wanted of him; finding himself wounded by love he can give no account of himself and stays astonied and ignorant.

SOUL: What is this arrow?

THE LORD: It is a spark of love which I send into man; it softens his hardness so that he melts like wax in the fire; and I give him the instinct to render to Me all the love I pour into him.

SOUL: What is this spark?

THE LORD: It is an inspiration sent by Me: like fire it sets ablaze man's heart, which takes from it such ardour and strength that he cannot do other than love. This love keeps man secretly attentive to Me, by means of My inspiration which warns him unceasingly that I am in his heart.

But what this inward inspiration is, which does such great things secretly, the tongue cannot say. Ask the heart which feels it; ask the understanding which understands it; ask the mind filled by this work, which God has wrought by means of heart, understanding and mind. Least of all can the tongue make it known. God fills man with love; He draws Him to Himself by love; by love He causes him to work mightily against the world, hell and himself. But this love is unknown and none can tell of it.

CHAPTER XIII

How love cannot understand itself, and how the heart filled with love lives contented. Of the great mercy shewn by God to man in this life. How His justice is seen at the moment when the soul, being separated from the body, goes to the place destined for it. How the soul cannot rest except in God.

O my heart, what wilt thou say of this love? What feelest thou?

I say, the joy within me speaks for me, but there

are no words to fit it. Not by outward signs, nor by martyrdoms, even suffered for love of God, can this love be understood. Only he who feels it can understand something of it. All that can be said of love is nothing; the further one advances in it, the less he knows of it. But this heart is still full and content; it neither seeks nor would find aught but what it feels. All love says is deep in the heart, full of savour, delightful; love's sayings are so subtle and secret, and so united with Him who inspires them, that the heart understands them only in secret and because it is united with God who alone understands. The heart feels but understands not, and thus this work is still in God while man's is the profit, and the loving and inmost way in which God works is still a secret between them, that is between God and the heart.

THE LORD: O Soul, what canst thou say of this work?

SOUL: I feel in myself a will so strong and lively, and so great a freedom, that I have no fear lest anything will come between me and my object, in which I content myself. A great light is shed on my understanding which every day grows more quiet. New things are shewn to it day by day, and works so delightful and loving that still to be busy with them contents it; it finds rest in them and can seek nought else, yet cannot say what are these works or how they are wrought. Memory is ever happy and busy over spiritual things so that it can hardly recall aught else, yet knows neither the means nor the form of its busyness. Affection, that is love, which is natural to man, says that it has been overshadowed by another and supernatural love to which alone it can attend, yet it is satisfied and happy, and neither wishes for other food nor seeks it, but seems to itself to have all it could want, nor can it tell the form of what satisfies it. Man has been conquered by a working beyond all his strength.

What more shall I say of this work of love? I cannot but hold my peace, yet, albeit I cannot say what I would,

an instinct urges me to speak. Let him who would
experience these things abstain from all evil (as Saint
Paul says). When man so abstains, God of His grace
forthwith sheds good on him, and makes his mind
believe, giving him so much love that he is lost, drowned,
changed, conquered. And although it may seem a
great thing to abstain from every kind of evil, yet he
who considered God's promises to man and His dili-
gent care to succour him and defend him against all
his enemies, could not be kept back by any obstacle
from doing anything for love of God. When man has
begun to walk in the right path, then he goes on, knowing that it is God who, by His gracious inspirations
and the love He sheds in our souls, does in us all the good
we do. The soul works almost without weariness because
of the sweet savour which God mingles with our weariness.
As for man, it is enough for him to do nought against
his conscience, for God thereupon inspires all the good
He would have him do. He gives him the instinct for
it and the strength, or he could do nothing good. He
gives him power and means, causing him to do all
things with the utmost delight, even what to others seems
great penance.

O what love, what kindness and what mercy God
shews to man in this miserable world! But justice appears
at the moment when the soul is separated from the
body: if then there be nothing to be cleansed, God
with His ardent and burning love receives the soul into
Himself, and in one instant it is changed and finds
itself in God, to be in Him without end; or else, at
that instant, it goes to Purgatory or Hell; all is as God
ordains; He sends each one to his place; each one bears
in himself the sentence of the judgment rendered and
condemns himself. And if souls did not find their way
to the place ordained by God, they would be in greater
torment, for they would be outside the divine ordinance; souls suffer less torment than they might because
His mercy is nowhere lacking. The soul was created

by God and for God and ordained by God and can find no rest except in God. By justice the souls in Hell are in God; if they were outside God they would suffer a far worse hell for God's ordinance would have been transgressed. He gives them a terrible instinct to go to the place ordained for them, and if they went not thither they would suffer a double pain; yet they go thither not that their pain may be less but because they are forced by God's sovereign order which cannot fail.

END OF THE DIALOGUE